PENGUIN BOOKS

MME SUN YAT-SEN

Jung Chang was born in Sichuan Province, China, in 1952 and studied English Language and Literature at Sichuan University. In 1978 she became one of the first Chinese after the Cultural Revolution to win a scholarship to study in the UK. After spending a year at Ealing College of Higher Education, she went on to obtain a Ph.D. in Linguistics at York University – the first person from the People's Republic of China to receive a doctorate from a British university. Immediately afterwards she worked on the major TV series about China *The Heart of the Dragon*, first screened in 1984. Since then she has become involved in a number of cultural, educational and business projects.

Jon Halliday has written extensively on east Asia. He is the author of *A Political History of Japanese Capitalism* (translated into Chinese, 1980); *Japanese Imperialism Today* (with Gavan McCormack, Penguin, 1973); *Sirk on Sirk*; and co-editor (with Peter Fuller) of *The Psychology of Gambling* (Penguin, 1977). He is preparing a history of the Korean War with Bruce Cumings.

LIVES OF MODERN WOMEN

General Editor: Emma Tennant

Lives of Modern Women is a series of short biographical portraits by distinguished writers of women whose ideas, struggles and creative talents have made a significant contribution to the way we think and live now.

It is hoped that both the fascination of comparing the aims, ideals, set-backs and achievements of those who confronted and contributed to a world in transition and the high quality of writing and insight will encourage the reader to delve further into the lives and work of some of this century's most extraordinary and necessary women.

Jung Chang with Jon Halliday

Mme Sun Yat-sen,

(Soong Ching-ling)

Penguin Books

Penguin Books Ltd, Harmondsworth, Middlesex, England
Viking Penguin Inc., 40 West 23rd Street, New York, New York 10010, U.S.A.
Penguin Books Australia Ltd, Ringwood, Victoria, Australia
Penguin Books Canada Limited, 2801 John Street, Markham, Ontario, Canada L3R 1B4
Penguin Books (N.Z.) Ltd, 182–190 Wairau Road, Auckland 10, New Zealand

First published 1986
Published simultaneously by Viking

Grateful acknowledgement is made to the following for permission to reprint previously
published material:
   M. E. Sharpe, Armonk, N. Y. 10504, and Joint Publishing Co., Hong Kong for
extracts from *Re-Encounters in China* © 1985 by Harold R. Isaacs. Reprinted by
permission.
   Random House, Inc. for extracts from *Last Chance in China: The World War II
Despatches of John S. Service*, edited by Joseph W. Esherick © 1974 by Random House,
Inc. Reprinted by permission.
   The Estate of Edgar Snow, c/o Robert P. Mills, New York for extracts from Journey
to the Beginning © 1958 by Edgar Snow. Reprinted by permission.
   Curtis Brown Ltd, New York for extracts from Personal History © 1934, 1935 by
Vincent Sheean. Reprinted by permission.
   Brandt and Brandt, New York for extracts from *The Soong Sisters* © 1941 by Emily
Hahn. Reprinted by permission.

Made and printed in Great Britain by
Richard Clay (The Chaucer Press) Ltd,
Bungay, Suffolk
Filmset in Monophoto Photina by
Northumberland Press Ltd,
Gateshead, Tyne and Wear

LCCCN: 85–052210

921
Sun

CONTENTS

170522

NOTE ON NAMES AND SPELLING

There are different ways of transliterating Chinese names into English. In our text we have used the forms of names most familiar in English-language texts. Where variant spellings occur in quotations, the form we have used follows in brackets.

All Chinese names are written with the surname first.

1912   With a classmate at school in Macon, Georgia, USA (New China Pictures Co.)

1923   On board the first aeroplane built in China, named 'Rosamonde' after Ching-ling's Christian name (New China Pictures Co.)

1923   With Sun Yat-sen on board a warship on the first anniversary of the escape from Canton (New China Pictures Co.)

December 1924   Ching-ling and Sun at Tientsin, three months before Sun's death (New China Pictures Co.)

January 1926   Ching-ling, then head of the Women's Department of the Kuomintang, with representatives of women's organizations at Canton (New China Pictures Co.)

September 1927   Crowds greet Ching-ling on arrival in Moscow at the start of her exile (New China Pictures Co.)

A very 'European' Ching-ling in exile in Europe (New China Pictures Co.)

February 1933   After lunch at Ching-ling's house in Shanghai (New China Pictures Co.)

Wartime Chungking   The three Soong sisters together (New China Pictures Co.)

1942 A reserved Ching-ling with Chiang Kai-shek and her two sisters in Chungking (courtesy of Helen Foster Snow)

1956 Ching-ling on an inspection tour in a minority area on the southern border (Wen-wu Publishing Co., Beijing)

November 1957 Ching-ling, the only non-Communist representative at the meeting of world Communist parties in Moscow, watches Mao sign the final declaration (New China Pictures Co.)

1960 With Mme Chou En-lai and Tsai Chang [Ts'ai C'ang], President of the All-China Women's Federation (New China Pictures Co.)

1981 Deng Xiaoping, Li Xiannian and Mme Chou En-lai pay their last respects to Ching-ling (New China Pictures Co.)

1893 27 January	Born in Shanghai, second daughter of Ni Kwei-tseng and Charlie Soong.
1900	*Eight foreign powers invade Peking.* Enters the McTyeire School for Girls, Shanghai.
1908	To the USA to study: first to Summit, New Jersey; then the Wesleyan College, Macon, Georgia.
1911 10 October	*The Revolution led by Sun Yat-sen founds the first Republic.*
1913	*Sun goes into exile in Japan.* Graduates from the Wesleyan College; meets Sun Yat-sen in Japan.
1915 25 October	Marries Sun in Tokyo.
1916	Leaves Japan for Shanghai with Sun.
1917	To Canton; first attempt at a Northern Expedition. *October Revolution in Russia.*
1918	To Shanghai. Her father dies.
1920	Returns to Canton. Prepares for the new Northern Expedition.
1921	*The Chinese Communist Party is founded.*
1922	Escapes from Canton.

1923	Returns to Canton; reorganization of the Kuomintang (the party founded by Sun).
1924	*Kuomintang–Communist co-operation, with Soviet help.*
	Elected head of the Women's Department of the Kuomintang.
1925	
12 March	Sun Yat-sen dies in Peking.
1926	To Wuhan with the Kuomintang government after the Northern Expedition takes the city.
1927	*The Kuomintang, under Chiang Kai-shek, breaks with the Communists.*
September	Exile in Russia.
	Mei-ling (her sister) marries Chiang Kai-shek.
December	To Brussels for an anti-imperialist conference; elected Honorary President.
1928	To Berlin.
May	Returns to China for Sun Yat-sen's official funeral
1929	at Nanking.
1930	Returns to Europe.
1931	Returns to Shanghai.
	Her mother dies.
	Japan attacks Mukden (Shenyang) and begins its occupation of Manchuria.
1932	Sets up the China League for Civil Rights.
1936	*The Sian Incident: Chiang Kai-shek is kidnapped.*
1937	*Sino-Japanese War. United Front between the Kuomintang and the Communists.*
	Leaves Shanghai for Hong Kong.
1938	Founds the China Defence League.
1940	To Chungking (the wartime Kuomintang capital) briefly with her sisters.
1941	Leaves Hong Kong for Chungking on the last plane

before the Japanese take Hong Kong.

1945   *The Sino–Japanese War ends.*
Leaves Chungking for Shanghai.
Re-organizes the China Defence League as the
China Welfare Fund.

1946   *The Civil War breaks out.*
Appeals for a coalition government.

1949   Turns down a leadership offer from the
Kuomintang.
Chiang and the Kuomintang to Taiwan.

1 October   *Founding of the People's Republic of China.*
Becomes Vice-President of the Central People's
Government Council; Honorary President of the
All-China Women's Federation (henceforth
continuously).

1950   *Korean War.*
Re-organizes the China Welfare Fund as the China
Welfare Institute.

1952   Founds the *China Reconstructs* magazine.
To Vienna for the Congress of Peoples for Peace.

1956   *China completes the 'socialist transformation'.*

1957   *'Anti-Rightist' campaign.*
To Moscow with Mao for the Conference of World
Communist Parties.

1958   *Great Leap Forward and People's Communes.*

1966   *Cultural Revolution.*
Attacked; then protected by premier Chou En-lai.
Long silence.

1971   *Lin Piao dies.*

1976   *Deaths of Chou En-lai and Mao Tse-tung.*
Arrest of 'Gang of Four'; end of Cultural Revolution.

1977   *Deng Xiaoping comes to power.*

1981
February   Publishes her last article.

15 May	Inducted into the Communist Party.
16 May	Named Honorary President of the People's Republic.
29 May	Dies of leukaemia in Peking.

ACKNOWLEDGEMENTS

We would like to thank the following people who knew Mme Sun Yat-sen for giving us their personal recollections of her: Rewi Alley, Percy Chen, Si-lan (Sylvia) Chen, Yolanda Chen, Israel Epstein, Emily Hahn, Dr George Hatem and Maggie Keswick; and several people who prefer to remain anonymous.

Delia Davin, Stephen Endicott, Han Su-yin, Michael Holroyd, Jay Leyda, David Pollard, John W. Powell and Diana Sheean gave generous help with references and contacts, as did the staff at Wide Angle Press, Hong Kong, and at the library of Hong Kong University.

Helen Foster Snow and Xinhua News Agency kindly made available photographs. We would also like to thank Dominique Bourgois for her help on this.

Catriona Luckhurst and Tony Lacey at Penguin read the first draft with despatch and were most helpful with critical comments, as was Francine Winham. We owe especial thanks to Emma Tennant for her enthusiasm in commissioning the project and for her encouragement throughout.

Our gratitude is due to Vanessa Green for typing the manuscript most carefully at very short notice.

Jung Chang would like especially to thank her husband, Chun-yee, for his inspiration, encouragement and perceptive comments.

J.C. & J.H.

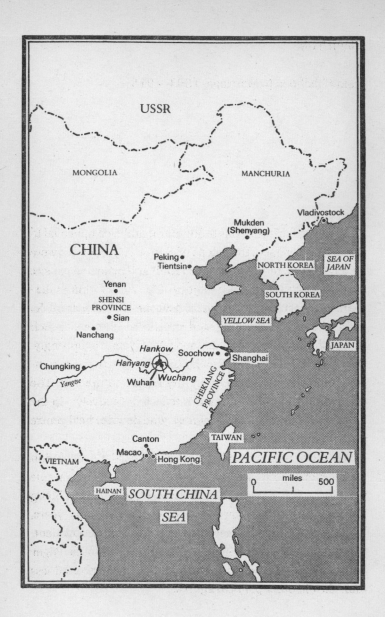

CHAPTER ONE

From Childhood to Marriage: 1893–1915

The twentieth century has brought unparalleled upheaval to China. As it opened, the troops of eight foreign powers were looting and burning the most beautiful and treasured palaces in the capital, Peking. For the next fifty years China underwent foreign invasions, colossal devastation and loss of life, bitter internecine fighting and drastic revolutions, which turned the country upside down repeatedly and agonizingly. Over the following three decades the new government changed Chinese society more than any regime in the past. The entire drama of modern China is reflected – actively – in the life of one woman, who for almost nine decades held centre stage: Soong Ching-ling.

Soong Ching-ling married the man who led the revolution which ended more than two thousand years of imperial rule in China – Sun Yat-sen. Her sister Mei-ling married Chiang Kai-shek, the right-wing leader of China for many years, while Ching-ling remained Chiang's staunchest opponent. She quite early sided with Mao Tse-tung, whom, as Edgar Snow reported her saying in the 1930s, she distrusted less than she did other political figures.

The unique eminence and unassailability of Soong Ching-ling is shown by the fact that she was called 'the Mother of China' by both the main political parties, the Communists and the Kuomintang, even though the two were bitter enemies. Just before her death she was named Honorary President of the People's Republic in Peking. She was praised by premier Chou En-lai as 'the jewel of the nation' – a remark which embodied the deep feelings of the Communist-oriented Chinese. The Kuomintang in Taiwan also revered her, but their reverence was tinged with awkwardness. Yet even they seemed to show respect for her adherence to her principles and her loyalty to her husband's ideals.

Soong Ching-ling was born on 27 January 1893, into a very unusual family. Both her parents were devout Christians in a non-Christian society. Her mother had, also most unusually, received a rather Westernized education; she was good at mathematics, and loved playing the piano. Ching-ling's father, known as Charlie Soong, had travelled abroad, first to Java as a boy, and then, in 1878, when he was twelve, to America. After some time in Boston, he ran away to sea and eventually ended up in North Carolina, among Southern Methodists, where he was baptized. He received a Methodist education in the American South, and then returned to Shanghai as an ordained minister in 1886. The following year he got married.

The combination of Christian and Western backgrounds made the life-style of Ching-ling's family a rare one for its time. Charlie gave up his missionary career soon after getting back to China and went into business as a comprador. He was the first agent for foreign machinery in Shanghai and soon became rich. At a time when most Chinese peasants had never seen a toothbrush, his Western-style house was replete with foreign-made facilities. Ching-ling later wrote to a friend in America:

> Our life here is exactly like yours. We live and dress à la European, even to the decoration of the rooms, so you can sometimes picture me not as a friend of faraway China, soaked in oriental atmosphere, but as one of your American friends in the busy city. For Shanghai is really very modern, more so than Atlanta in many ways. Our house is nice and big, and has all the modern conveniences. There are plenty of bedrooms and tubs and lavatories, so you must come for a visit some time.

Their bathrooms had 'pretty Soochow tubs with yellow dragons coiling round the outside and green glaze inside'. Charlie did things like digging the garden himself, thus rather shocking his genteel Chinese neighbours.

Ching-ling was the second of six children and the middle one of three sisters. The family has since become probably the most famous in China, particularly because of the destinies of the three sisters. Ai-ling, the eldest, who was born in 1890, married H. H. Kung, a direct descendant of Confucius, and later the Kuomintang Finance Minister – and she became reputedly the richest woman in China in her day, by combining genuine financial skill with unscrupulous use of inside knowledge. Mei-ling, several years younger than Ching-ling, made a much-publicized marriage with Chiang Kai-shek.

The different paths of the three sisters emerged out of identical family and almost identical educational backgrounds. Perhaps as a result of not having gone through a tough Chinese education themselves, their parents took a relatively relaxed attitude towards conventional Chinese learning. They sent their daughters to the leading foreign missionary school in Shanghai, the McTyeire School for Girls, and later to America. The sisters were the first Chinese girls to be educated in the USA.

Yet, in the very same environment as her two sisters, who remained life-long conservatives, even as a young child Ching-ling showed signs of a quite different character which made her into what the media called 'the Joan of Arc of China'.

Later in life Ching-ling joined forces with the man who in many ways was the most iconoclastic figure in Chinese politics, Mao Tse-tung. Signs of her independent spirit, foreshadowing this later alliance, can be seen in her time at McTyeire. Every Thursday evening there was a religious discussion at the school; Ching-ling often asked the pastor daring questions. Mei-ling was shocked. Once she reproached her sister indignantly: 'Why do you ask questions? Don't you believe?'

But there were other sides to Ching-ling. Though serious and inquisitive, she none the less was given the nick-name 'Little Pigtail' (Xiao Bian) at school. In Chinese this is quite a term of endearment and it is a name usually given to someone who is sweet and quiet, but also capable of being playful.

While Ching-ling was growing up in this rather Western environment round the turn of the century, conditions in China were deteriorating rapidly. The Ching imperial court, which had ruled the country for over two and a half centuries, had become, as Ching-ling herself described it in an essay published in 1912, 'a dynasty whose cruel extortions and selfishness [had] reduced the once prosperous nation to a poverty-stricken country'. She also attacked 'the most barbaric customs and degrading morals' of the court.

The court was particularly ineffective in resisting foreign pressure, at a time when this was escalating sharply. From around the end of the first half of the nineteenth century Western powers encroached more and more on China. Britain took the lead, inundating China with opium and seizing the first major colony, Hong Kong Island, in 1842. Over the next sixty years Britain expanded its colonial holdings, and other foreign powers – France, Russia, Germany and Japan – also seized territory and concessions. The attitude of the Western powers was summed up by Lord Rosebery: 'There we have a sick man worth many Turkeys, of more value to us as a people than all the Armenians that ever walked the earth; as a commercial inheritance priceless, beyond all the ivory and peacocks that ever came out of Africa.'

The Ching court's ignorance of the outside world was staggering. In 1900, when eight foreign powers invaded Peking, a senior court official actually suggested to the Dowager Empress that to defeat the foreigners all the Chinese had to do was to hit the backs of their knees with bamboo sticks so that they would fall down and never be able to get up again, as foreigners could not bend their knees. Under guidance of this sort, China was defeated over and over again. After much humiliation, and the loss of extensive territory, as well as national sovereignty and economic rights, it became clear that the court was rotten to the core and incapable of effecting reform from within. A revolution to overthrow the Ching became the choice of many radicals. The man who came to lead the revolution was Ching-ling's future husband, Sun Yat-sen.

Sun was born into a very poor peasant family in Kwangtung, south China. As a teenager, he went to a British missionary school in Hawaii, was later baptized, and acquired a first-class medical qualification in Hong Kong and practised as a doctor in Macao. Within two years of opening up his practice as a doctor, Sun turned from the curing of physical illness on an individual level to the human and social illnesses of the Chinese nation of 400 million people. One of the factors which contributed to this move was his poverty-stricken background, which Ching-ling later described:

Many times Sun Yat-sen told me that it was in those early days, as a poor son of a poor peasant family, that he became a revolutionary. He was determined that the lot of the Chinese peasant should not continue to be so wretched, that little boys in China should have shoes to wear and rice to eat. For this ideal he gave forty years of his life.

It was the awareness provided by travelling overseas which broadened Sun's horizons and stimulated his revolutionary commitment. Paradoxically as it might now seem, one aspect of this was his experience in Hong Kong. In one of his speeches Sun talked with enthusiasm of the 'clean' politics, administration and social appearance of the island under British rule, and contrasted this with the corruption of the Ching government. He went on: 'Once I was asked where and how I got my revolutionary ideas. I would like to reply frankly that my revolutionary ideas came from Hong Kong.' Like most other Chinese revolutionary leaders, he was much impressed by Western technology and political and social systems and sought to learn from the West so that China would be able to stand up to it. The target of revolution was always, first and foremost, China's own rulers.

The interaction of national factors and international intervention crystallized for Sun in 1894 when Japan attacked China. In that year Sun founded his first revolutionary organization, the Revive China Society, in Hawaii. The next year he returned to China and organized the first of his revolutionary uprisings, reportedly after receiving a message from Charlie Soong from Shanghai, urging him to take advantage of the disgust with the Ching court created in the aftermath of China's defeat in the Sino-Japanese War of 1894–5. Sun's 1895 attempt was a failure. The Ching put a price of 1,000 silver dollars on his head, and he had to flee to Hawaii again. Over the next fifteen years Sun's life was constantly in danger and he had to live a nomadic exile's life.

In October 1896 he had a particularly close shave in London when he was kidnapped and detained in the Chinese Legation in Portland Place for twelve days. As so often, Sun used his extraordinary powers of persuasion to get himself out of a seemingly hopeless situation. He persuaded two employees of the Legation to smuggle messages out to his former teacher and friend Dr James Cantlie, who lived round the corner from the Legation in Devonshire Place. These messages saved Sun from death and worse. It was unlikely that such a prestigious leader would be lucky enough to be beheaded. Sun's courage can easily be seen from the description of the death which he himself anticipated:

First having my ankles crushed in a vice and broken by a hammer, my eyelids cut off, and finally being chopped to small fragments, so that none could claim my mortal remains. For the old Chinese code does not err on the side of mercy to political offenders.

For most of the period between 1895 and 1911 Sun was forced to stay abroad. He made only a few clandestine visits to China. When he was in Shanghai he usually stayed with Charlie Soong, who had become a close and trusted colleague. Charlie Soong played a major role in financing Sun's political activities and in securing business support for him. Among his other activities, Charlie had founded a publishing house where he printed bibles and used this as a cover for printing Sun's revolutionary pamphlets. The Soong children looked on Sun like a member of the family and took to him. Perhaps they were not too young to guess something of Sun's importance from his fleeting visits and the reaction of their father.

However, Ching-ling *was* too young to join the revolution in person. In 1908, at the age of fifteen, she was sent away to school in America, first to Summit, New Jersey, and then to Wesleyan College in Macon, Georgia. She and her sisters were the first Chinese most people there had ever met. Although not, apparently, overtly discriminated against herself, she did feel deeply about the general discrimination against Asians and the ill-treatment of blacks in the American South. Many years later, talking to Edgar Snow, she was to contrast this, somewhat schematically, with attitudes in Russia: 'The Russians don't treat colored people as racial inferiors. Americans won't let colored boys and girls go to school with their children, and yet they call themselves Christians.' In spite of all this, she seems to have kept a strong sentimental attachment to Wesleyan. In 1976, more than sixty years after she graduated, she sent the college a wall-hanging as a present. She always preferred friends to call her by her Wesleyan nickname, Suzie, and also liked the Christian name she had at that time, Rosamonde.

Yet, with all this, Ching-ling did not immerse herself in the atmosphere of the United States. She remained very Chinese, unlike her younger sister, Mei-ling, who said of herself: 'The only thing Oriental about me is my face.' Ching-ling seems to have had difficulty adopting American idioms and customs.

Ching-ling is remembered as a very popular pupil at the school – gentle, thoughtful and sensitive. She went out of her way to help friends, and kept her friendships. She majored in philosophy and was also, for a time, literary editor of the school magazine. As at McTyeire in Shanghai, she was hard-working and deeply involved with big issues – China's destiny and world affairs.

At the age of eighteen she wrote an essay for the college magazine, the *Wesleyan*, entitled 'The Influence of Foreign-Educated Students on China'. Ching-ling's desire for the reform of her country, 'that ancient contemporary of Egypt, Babylonia and Assyria', bursts off the page. One can feel her youthful enthusiasm for the role of the returned students – doubtless she saw herself in the same role once she had finished her education in America. In this essay her model of a revitalized nation was entirely Western. She seemed to have an almost dream-like vision of Western nations. She refers to such novelties as the introduction of 'the science of government' into China and suggests that the ethical standards of Chinese officials had been improved by the example of returned students. Ching-ling also notes that the foreign-educated students introduced 'Western athletics and gymnastics' – another major novelty, since strenuous bodily movement had been frowned upon as unsuitable for genteel scholars.

Ching-ling's approach to revolution then was a non-violent one. She invoked the ideals of Liberty and Equality which, she wrote, 'are not secured by strikes, riots and political disturbances, but by more general education and enlightenment'. Yet, more than this was to be needed to change China, and Ching-ling's ideas, too, were to change, as was her image of the West – however, this happened not in Georgia, but in her own long and turbulent experience in Canton, Shanghai and Peking.

One thing she singled out was arranged marriage. At the time, this was standard practice throughout Chinese society. Married couples betrothed their offspring not just when they were approaching marriageable age, but often as very young children, or even before they were born – so-called 'womb engagements',* entered into during pregnancy. At the age of eighteen Ching-ling tackled this institution with the same Western-initiated sense of emancipation with which she embarked on her own marriage a few years later. She also approached the question in a way which united the issues of 'women's liberation' and 'men's liberation': for her the

---

* In Chinese: *zhi* [point] *fu* [belly] *wei* [become] *hun* [marriage]

abolition of arranged marriage would further the liberation of both men and women.

Ching-ling's essay is ebullient, and full of hope. At a time when it was easy to be narrowly nationalistic, her vision, like Sun Yat-sen's, was firmly centred on China's interests, but not at all xenophobic. It seems to have been the combination of the relative freedom in the USA (even in deepest Georgia) and the rapidly exploding situation in China which catalysed Ching-ling's feelings for her country and her people and set her on her life-long path which was to stretch, unbroken, seventy years into the future.

By the time Ching-ling had published this essay China had seen a number of uprisings. Sun Yat-sen later said of his endeavours, tidily rounding the figure in a typical Chinese way, that up till October 1911 he had had ten failures. But the eleventh attempt was a success – and one with epochal significance: it brought over two thousand years of imperial rule – and misrule – to an end.

Strangely, this crucial event met with relatively easy initial success. The uprising first broke out in the city of Wuchang, in central China, on 10 October (since known as the 'Double 10th'). It was detonated by the chance discovery of some explosives belonging to revolutionaries, which forced the uprising to start prematurely. But it met with strong support from local troops and within twenty-four hours the city of Wuchang was taken. Events moved so fast that the revolutionaries had no leader – Sun Yat-sen was still abroad. So they decided to invite a colonel in the Ching army, Li Yuan-hung, *pro tempore*, and sent a delegation to Li's house. Li, thinking they wanted to kill him, ran from room to room, patiently followed by the deputation. Finally Li hid under his wife's bed, but left one foot visible. The deputation grabbed his foot and pulled him out. As Li began to plead for his life, the head of the deputation politely asked after his health. And then, wisely elevating his rank, said: 'General Li, we should be greatly honoured if you and your troops would join our ranks.' Li, now with the rank of Generalissimo, issued a rather optimistic proclamation announcing the overthrow of the Ching dynasty and the establishment of a revolutionary military government. The revolution was so popular that this single spark started a prairie fire. Within two months, seventeen provinces successively proclaimed their independence from the Ching. Ching rule collapsed. In Sun Yat-sen's words: 'And so heaven itself helped China.'

Sun's paramount importance in the whole revolution is shown by the fact that although he was not even in China at the time, he was the unchallenged choice for President of the new Republic. News of the success reached Sun as he was travelling on a fund-raising tour in the USA. Characteristically, he decided not to interrupt his tour, even to become President. From America he went on to England. Another telegram reached him there, reiterating the invitation to become President, after it was inadvertently delivered to the Chinese (i.e. Ching) Legation. Dr Cantlie, his old friend, asked him if he would now accept: 'Yes,' replied Sun, 'for the time being, if no-one else can be found better in the meantime.'

Sun did not get back to China until Christmas Day 1911. He was sworn in as the first Provisional President at Nanking on 1 January 1912. All the members of the Soong family who were in China at the time were present. When the news reached Ching-ling in Georgia, she immediately put pen to paper and wrote 'The Greatest Event of the Twentieth Century'.

This essay overflows with a tremendous sense of pride in her country's achievements. China at last was to be lifted from the bottom place to the rank which its history and culture merited in the world. Her exuberance found typically Chinese expression: she lavished praise on the country's great cultural heritage, as well as on its sheer size: 'A race amounting to one-quarter of the world's population, and inhabiting the largest empire of the globe, whose civilization displays so many manifestations of excellence ... her extensive literature ... and her exquisite code of Social and Moral ethics are hardly paralleled elsewhere.' Foreigners are proudly quoted, as the Chinese tend to place special, perhaps excessive, importance on how they are viewed by almost any foreigner. Ching-ling quoted not only Napoleon ('When China moves, she will move the world'), but also the favourable words of a former American Minister to China.

Ching-ling began to plan her country's immediate future: 'Since order is restored, the Currency Problem and the Taxation Question will be the next problem to be solved.' And she moved on to the future of the world: 'Universal Peace – when Rights need not be backed by armies and "dreadnoughts," and all political disagreements will be, at last, settled by the Hague Tribunal.'

Ching-ling believed wholeheartedly in the possibility of changing the world, in an innocent, naïve and passionate way. In China it is believed that a truly great person is one who, as the sage Mencius put it, never loses the heart of a child. And this unreserved optimism was soon to mesh with that of another person with the 'heart of a child' – Sun Yat-sen.

It was in this spirit that Sun took the amazing decision to step down as President after barely one month in office, in favour of the powerful military commander Yuan Shih-kai – on condition that Yuan got the Emperor to abdicate to avoid bloodshed and organized a Republican government. The Emperor resigned on 12 February 1912, and Sun did so the following day. His already dominant personality acquired even greater moral prestige.

So when Ching-ling graduated the next year, 1913, she was full of excitement at the prospect of meeting Sun Yat-sen again. She wrote to one of her teachers: 'I shall soon be on my way home ... I am taking a box of California fruit to Dr Sun from his admirers here, and I am also the proud bearer of a private letter to him.'

Meanwhile, Charlie Soong was working closely with Sun Yat-sen, acting as his treasurer. Sun soon broke with Yuan Shih-kai because Yuan was only paying lip-service to the principles of the Republic. After an abortive revolution against Yuan in 1913 Sun was forced to go into exile again in Japan.

It was during this period of exile in Japan that the lives of both Sun Yat-sen and Soong Ching-ling went through a dramatic change: on 25 October 1915 the two were married in Tokyo. He was forty-nine; she was twenty-two.

For Ching-ling, as she told Edgar Snow many years later: 'It was hero-worship from afar.' In a typically Chinese under-stated way she said: 'It was a romantic girl's idea when I ran away to work for him – but a good one. I wanted to help save China and Dr Sun was the one man who could do it. So I wanted to help him.' For the Chinese it is not only honourable, but also admirable for a girl to worship the hero of a great cause and to want to marry him.

However, Sun was already married, with three children. This had been an arranged marriage, and took place when Sun was nineteen. Prior to the wedding ceremony, the couple had never set eyes on each other, and had no say in the matter. Three months after the wedding, Sun went back to Hong Kong to resume his studies, and since then had been living apart from his wife, whom he saw only very occasionally. He was leading a precarious and unsettled exile's life, and left his wife and children in the care of his brother in Hawaii. Mrs Sun was an outsider to Sun's cause, and did not share his work. But she was an unfailingly devoted wife, a good mother and a dutiful daughter-in-law. The relationship was a very common one in China then: a couple bound together by fate and the decisions of others, fulfilling their duty untiringly, with little to say to each other, like two parallel lines which never meet. Most people hardly gave a thought to whether this was the kind of relationship they wanted. It was just a way of life that had been going on for thousands of years and was taken for granted.

At the age of forty-nine Sun had never experienced deep emotional involvement. Suddenly Ching-ling appeared, young, vivacious and beautiful. She was completely dedicated to him, with unreserved enthusiasm for his cause. What is more, she understood and shared his plans, desires and dreams.

At the beginning of the century there was no such thing in China as formal divorce in the generally understood present-day sense of the term. Sun had two alternatives. One was to take Ching-ling as a concubine. The other was to dismiss his wife with a reason which would have involved great humiliation for her. Clearly both were impossible. So what happened is that Sun and his wife created a sort of precedent in Chinese marriage practice, by coming to an amicable arrangement for a permanent separation.

Not everybody welcomed this agreement with open arms. At first, Ching-ling's parents disapproved strongly of her marriage, which in a sense was tantamount to an elopement. Ching-ling later told Edgar Snow: 'My parents . . . tried to lock me up. I climbed out the window and escaped with the help of my amah.'

The marriage was a sensation, particularly in a society like China, which was a hot-bed for gossip, rumours and legends. Christians, who strongly opposed divorce, were especially critical of the marriage. Also strongly against it were some *bien pensant* members of society, who thought Sun should only leave his wife if she had been at fault; all knew this not to be the case with Mrs Sun. Some of Sun's friends also worried that it might tarnish his moral image – and therefore the cause, too. Lastly, Sun's foes naturally latched on to the issue, criticizing both Sun and Ching-ling, whom they called an adventuress.

But positive reactions were much stronger. Radicals, especially the young, warmly welcomed the marriage. First of all, it defied feudal tradition. Second, by running away from home to be with the man she loved, Ching-ling gave a big boost to women's liberation. In addition, her act was justified by some as being in the line of a great Chinese romantic tradition (at least as it appears in literature and historical legend) of a woman's right to pursue love. And, which must not be underestimated, there was the almost magical appeal which Ching-ling had for the Chinese. This was in part simply to do with her looks. To the Chinese she had perfectly formed features, suggesting nobility, dignity and inner depth – the face and stature of a princess. Her magical appeal was described by Mme Chou En-lai in her funeral valedictory:

I remember the winter of 1924 when you accompanied Dr Sun Yat-sen to Tianjin [Tientsin]. You came up on the ship's deck to face the welcoming throng. I, standing among them, saw Dr Sun ... standing straight and firm, although age and illness already marked his face ... And on his right, I saw you – erect, slim, graceful, young, beautiful, dignified, tranquil, inspired by revolutionary ideals. As an image of a young woman revolutionary, you remained clearly in my mind from then on.

These qualities seemed to the Chinese to provide the right kind of image for the wife of the nation's revolutionary leader. And marrying Sun while he was in exile, rather than in power, was seen as further proof that Ching-ling was not after personal advantage, and as a sign of devotion to the revolutionary cause.

Last but not least, was she not the daughter of Charlie Soong, Sun Yat-sen's closest colleague and old friend? Such a woman could not be an adventuress. In fact, her parents' initial disapproval later evaporated. They gave her a tra-ditional Chinese wedding present – a brocade embroidered with one hundred sons.

The sensation soon died down and most of China welcomed Ching-ling warmly as a worthy and dignified 'first lady', who more than earned the right to inherit the respect and devotion which had attached to Sun Yat-sen. Some years after Sun Yat-sen died in 1925, Edgar Snow asked Ching-ling which of her achievements meant most to her: ' "The fact that I was loyal to Dr Sun from the day I met him until his death," she answered without hesitation. "I still am." '

The marriage to Sun threw Ching-ling into the centre of the whirlpool of Chinese politics and set her on the course of her stormy life. As Mme Sun she acquired a form of invulnerability, but she also earned it in her own right, by never faltering in courage or in her devotion to the principles which Sun espoused.

CHAPTER TWO

'First Lady' of China: 1915–25

Ching-ling's marriage to Sun Yat-sen was to last only ten years. On 12 March 1925 Sun died of cancer, in Peking.

The decade of their marriage was one of constant turmoil and movement in Chinese political life, and in their life as a couple. Sun was in and out of power and both Sun and Ching-ling were in and out of danger. Years later Ching-ling told Han Su-yin of an episode right at the beginning of their married life: 'I remember that last time he returned from Japan ... We stayed in disguise in Shanghai, in the garret of a French newspaperman's house. We never went out in the daytime, only by night, and even then, we were heavily disguised.'

Through all this Ching-ling seems to have enjoyed a very happy marriage with Sun. Soon after the wedding she wrote to a friend who had been at school with her in America: 'I am happy and try to help my husband as much as possible with his English correspondence. My French has greatly improved and I am now able to read French papers and translate by sight easily. So you see marriage for me is like going to school except that there are no "exams" to trouble me.' Ching-ling worked as Sun's interpreter, cryptographer and closest political adviser.

Sun's bodyguard, Morris ('Two-Gun') Cohen, had no doubt about Ching-ling's role: 'The most important member of the staff was Mme Sun herself. She never interfered during his office hours, but it was she alone who made his life possible by keeping him cheerful and happy no matter what went on.' They spent every evening together 'reading and chatting'. In spite of Sun's reputation for being 'dead serious', he did relax as well. Ching-ling occasionally put on a private film show for him. And they had a croquet lawn in the garden at Shanghai. Sun Yat-sen would swing his mallet and send Ching-ling's ball to the very edge of the lawn at the first chance he got. She would turn to the friends looking on and yell out: 'Watch that Bolshevik.'

Ching-ling also had to adapt to public life. She wrote to a friend in America:

> You know how I dread publicity! But since my marriage I have had to participate in many affairs which I'd otherwise escape. The Chinese are not like Europeans. They always thrust greatness and honour, not upon those who deserve them, but upon the timid. I see people every day; in fact I'm simply pulled out of my shell by circumstances. I was dumbfounded at some of the reports that have been manufactured about me in Macon. For instance, I learned that I was once a spy of the revolutionists before my marriage! And the various exciting and thrilling incidents that I have gone through must have been my nightmares, though I'm sure I *never* told about them!

It is easy to forget what a stunning departure Ching-ling's role was within Chinese culture. Up till then Chinese women had been virtually invisible: most urban women had bound feet; they were kept at home; they never showed their faces in public. Wives were never seen with their husbands on any social occasions, which were for men only. Ching-ling was the first Chinese woman to appear in public with her husband. At almost all gatherings she was the only woman present. What is more, she was not just his spouse – she was a full political colleague. In fact, she was the first consort of a political leader anywhere in the world to act as 'first lady'. She not only long predated Eleanor Roosevelt, but also far outshone her in political importance.

Ching-ling's new life began in exile in Japan, at a time when the Chinese government was headed by Sun's arch-enemy, Yuan Shih-kai.

In December 1915 Yuan declared himself Emperor. Six months later, in June 1916, he dropped dead. The Suns were able to return openly to Shanghai and from the summer of 1916 settled down in a modest house in the rue Molière in the French Concession.

Ever since the fall of the Ching, China had been riven by feuding military factions headed by warlords, usually controlling only a small part of the country. By and large, the warlords were more powerful in northern China – hence Sun was more active in southern China.

In mid-1917 Sun was welcomed to Canton and elected head of a new republican military government, with the high-sounding title of Grand Marshal, or Generalissimo.

He had earlier founded a revolutionary party, the Kuomintang (Nationalist Party). And from now on he and his party were to use Canton as the base to try to unify China. They launched a series of 'Northern Expeditions' to oust the war-lords, who had a form of government in the north.

In spite of his grand plans, and his grand title, Sun was in fact the prisoner of a group of militarists in Canton. In April 1918 he lost his title of Generalissimo. In May he had to resign. He returned to Shanghai with Ching-ling. Ching-ling got back just in time to be at her father's bedside when he died, on 3 May 1918, at the age of only fifty-two.

The Suns stayed for the next two years in Shanghai, where Ching-ling and Sun worked on producing published versions of Sun's addresses and articles. This was no easy task. Sun had to appeal to a vast constituency. Ching-ling told Edgar Snow:

> He spoke conservatively to those whose help he needed, and his books were edited so as not to divide his followers. 'We have to be very careful how we go at things,' he was always warning me. 'Do it the Chinese way – roundabout – never directly at the goal.'

And, talking about his lectures: 'Ching-ling smiled and threw back her head. "He made it all up on the spur of the moment. It all depended on the political situation and the audience. I would be nervous as a cat, sitting next to him on the platform and wondering what was coming next." ' There is plenty of room for thinking that Ching-ling both put some order in Sun's sometimes woolly ideas and helped urge him to a more radical position later in life.

After these two quiet years Ching-ling and Sun suddenly found themselves heading back for Canton. In October 1920 an ally of Sun's seized power there and invited the Suns to return.

In the meantime events were taking place elsewhere in China which were to have a decisive influence on the country's history – and on the thought and action of both Sun and Ching-ling.

In July 1921 the Chinese Communist Party was founded in Shanghai. Among those attending was Mao Tse-tung. The man who was elected Secretary-General, Chen Tu-hsiu, was not there, but in Canton, working with Sun Yat-sen. Chen, the leading Marxist intellectual in the country, was given the post of Commissioner of Education – the first Marxist ever to hold a post in a Chinese government. By making this appointment, Sun was, among other things, able to balance his regime against pressures from the more conservative elements in the Kuomintang.

While Sun had wanted Canton as a base for a Northern Expedition, the Canton merchants were unhappy at seeing their funds 'diverted' for an attempt to unify the country. An uprising was organized against Sun. On 15 June 1922 troops opened fire on the guards at the Suns' residence. Quite clearly they had not been expecting this. Ching-ling's sister Ai-ling had been staying with the Suns until two days before, with her baby daughter Rosamonde (named after one of Ching-ling's two American names). Ching-ling had even asked Ai-ling to leave her daughter behind for a while with her (Ching-ling) in Canton.

Ching-ling herself has left a vivid account of 'The Escape from Canton', which many Chinese thought a classic. It is the only description she ever published about the sort of dangers she went through.

*

About two o'clock on the morning of June 16th Dr Sun roused me from my sweet dreams, telling me to hurry and dress, that we were in danger and must escape ...

I thought it would be inconvenient for him to have a woman along with him, and urged him to leave me behind for the time being. There couldn't, I said, be much danger for me as a private person. At last he saw the sense of my argument, but he would not go even then until he had left all fifty of our bodyguard to protect the house. Then he departed alone.

Half an hour after he had gone ... rifle shots rang out in the vicinity ...

The enemy fired downhill at us from two sides, shouting, 'Kill Sun Wen [Yat-sen]! Kill Sun Wen!' Pitch darkness covered them completely. Our small defence corps therefore kept quiet. I could just discern the crouching bodies of our guards in the darkness.

As day broke our men began to reply to the fire with their rifles and machine guns, while the enemy employed field guns. My bath was smashed to bits. One-third of our handful of troops had been wiped out, but the remaining men resisted with more determination than ever. One of the servants climbed to a high place and succeeded in killing quite a number of the enemy. By eight o'clock our store of ammunition was running low, so we decided to stop shooting and preserve what was left until the last possible moment.

There seemed no use in remaining now. Our Captain advised me to leave and the troops agreed with him, promising for their part to stay there in order to halt any possible pursuit by the enemy ... Later, all of the fifty were reported killed.

Four of us, Colonel Bow, who was a foreign attendant of Dr Sun's, two of the guards and myself, taking with us only the most necessary supplies for every day, crawled along the bridge passage to make our escape. The enemy soon concentrated fire on this passage and flying bullets whistled about our ears. Twice bullets brushed past my temple without injuring me ...

From eight in the morning till four that afternoon we were literally buried in a hell of constant gunfire. Bullets flew in all directions. Once the entire ceiling of a room I had left only a few minutes before collapsed.

At four o'clock Division-commander Wei Pang-ping, who had until then been neutral, sent down an officer to talk peace with us and to offer conditions of surrender. The first demand made by our guard was for my safety, which the officer refused to guarantee, saying that they had no power over the troops of another man. Even the enemy officers could do nothing with these soldiers, who had by this time gone completely mad. Our iron gates were soon smashed and we were confronted by the bloodthirsty bayonets and revolvers of the soldiers, who rushed, however, not for our persons but for the bundles in our hands. Quickly we seized our chance, and ran toward two currents of wild crowds of troops, rushing into each other's paths; one was a group of escaping soldiers and the other a batch of enemy looters. I succeeded in making an escape, wearing Colonel Bow's hat and Dr Sun's raincoat.

... I was absolutely exhausted, and begged the guards to shoot me. Instead they dragged me forward, one on each side supporting me ... Corpses lay about everywhere, some of the Party people and others of plain citizens. Their chests were caved in, their arms slashed, their legs severed. Once we saw two men squatting face to face under a roof. Closer observation revealed that they were dead, their eyes wide open. They must have been killed by stray bullets.

Again our way was cut off by a group of the mob running out of a little passage. The whisper ran through our party that we should lie flat in the street, pretending to be dead. In this way we were left unmolested; then we arose and continued our journey. My guards advised me to avoid looking at the corpses lest I should faint. Half an hour later, when the rifle shots were thinning out, we came to a small farmhouse. The owner tried to drive us out, fearing the consequences of sheltering us; his attempt was forestalled, however, by a timely swoon on my part.

I woke up to find the guards washing me with cold water, and fanning me. One of them went out to see what he could of the way things were going, when suddenly there came a tattoo of rifle shots. The guard indoors rushed to shut the door; he told me that the other one had been struck by a bullet and was probably dead by this time.

While the firing subsided I disguised myself as an old countrywoman, and with the guard in the guise of a pedlar we left the cottage. I picked up a basket and a few vegetables on the way, and carried them with me. At last we reached the house of a friend which had already been searched that morning. To go on was absolutely impossible, so we spent the night there. Shelling never ceased the entire night, and our relief was enormous when we heard cannon shots at last from the gunboats. Dr Sun, then, was safe ...

Next morning, still in my countrywoman outfit, I arrived

at Shameen with the others, and there another friend, a foundry worker, arranged for a small motor-boat for me, by which we got to another house in Linnan. The river was thronged with boats full of booty, both girls and goods. They were being sent away for safety. It was reported that two women unfortunate enough to answer to my description had been thrown into jail. That same afternoon I left Canton; the house in which I had stayed the night was searched again.

At last, that night, I succeeded in meeting Dr Sun on board ship, after a life-and-death struggle. We soon went to Hongkong, disguised.

In the escape Ching-ling, who was pregnant, had a miscarriage and lost her only child.

The couple then left Hong Kong and moved back to Shanghai.

Events had been moving fast both within China and in the outside world. Abroad, the Bolshevik Revolution had consolidated itself and was taking an active interest in China, and Ching-ling and Sun increasingly looked to Bolshevism for alternatives. The Suns' shift was stimulated by increasing disillusionment with the Western powers. Ching-ling told Edgar Snow:

'After the republic was set up the foreign powers still ran China like a colony. Dr Sun tried again and again to get aid in London, Washington and Paris to carry out his plans for the international development of China. He was always treated contemptuously, laughed at and turned away.'

'Russia was his last chance?'

'You might say his last choice.'

When Snow asked her: '... he never did believe in Communism?', Ching-ling replied: 'Oh, yes! But not at first. He thought our revolution should follow a different path from Russia's. After 1923, however, he believed we could travel the same road.'

At a time when the Western powers were treating China with contempt, the new Soviet regime was behaving with generosity and tact. Its first and spectacular gesture was the unilateral renunciation announced in 1919 of all Tsarist privileges in China. To the Suns and the Chinese people nothing could mean more than this. The Chinese Communist Party also evolved a co-operative approach. In August 1922 one of its heads, Li Ta-chao, met Ching-ling and Sun in Shanghai and proposed that he (Li) join the Kuomintang. Sun agreed that Communists should be enrolled as individuals in the Kuomintang – they had common enemies: the warlords at home and the imperialists from abroad. This was the beginning of a close organizational relationship which was to last until Chiang Kai-shek shattered the coalition after Sun's death. The agreement marked the start of a movement which has continued throughout China's recent history: the trend towards unity between all forces capable of uniting behind a national programme. There have so far been two periods of Communist–Kuomintang co-operation: the first lasted from 1922/3 to 1927; the second from 1937 to 1945/6. The People's Republic is currently calling for a third – to reunite Taiwan with the mainland. In traditional Chinese philosophy opposition and unity are viewed as inevitably superseding each other in turn.

The chance for Sun's Kuomintang to put its new strategy

into effect came very quickly. In February 1923 troops favourable to Sun retook Canton and Sun and Ching-ling returned there on 21 February, hailed by vast crowds. Ching-ling played a major role in reorganizing the Kuomintang and in the shift away from the Western powers towards Russia. In an interview with *The New York Times* in July 1923 Sun said he had lost all faith in the Western powers and trusted no one but the Russians.

In August, Sun sent a mission to Moscow, headed by the then little-known Chiang Kai-shek, a man with very close ties to the Shanghai underworld and business. Chiang was so impressed with Soviet training that he later arranged for large numbers of young cadres from his province, Chekiang, to be trained in Russia, as well as his eldest son, Ching-kuo, the present head of Taiwan, who spent eleven years there and acquired both fluent Russian and a Russian wife. (Chiang later sent his second son to study in Nazi Germany.)

Meanwhile, an envoy came from Moscow – the able figure of Mikhail Borodin, not long out of Glasgow's Barlinnie prison. As chief political adviser, Borodin supervised the reorganization of the Kuomintang along Soviet party lines. Ching-ling was an active participant in the negotiations with Borodin on this issue.

In January 1924 Sun convened a special Congress to reorganize the Kuomintang. Ching-ling was one of the 199 delegates, along with Ho Hsiang-ning, the wife of Liao Chung-kai, the left-wing Kuomintang leader (and one other woman). They were the first women ever to be elected to senior positions in any political organization – or indeed any organization *tout court* – in China's history. Ching-ling was made head of the

Women's Department of the Party. Her view was that Chinese women's liberation was an inseparable part of the Chinese revolution. She was opposed to the view that women's liberation was antithetical to the liberation of men; the two had to go together. Therefore, there was no separate women's movement like the suffragettes in Britain. Ching-ling's views set the tone henceforth for the radical line on the question of women in China.

The most important feature of the Congress was the adoption of the policies of alliance with the Soviet Union and the (Chinese) Communist party. Three members of the Communist Party, including Li Ta-chao, were elected to the Central Committee; and six others, including Mao Tse-tung, became alternate members. Mao was made the first head of the Propaganda Department. Much later, in 1940, Mao singled out this Congress as a key moment in China's history, and reminded his readers that, as a Kuomintang member, he had personally witnessed the adoption of the new programme.

Ching-ling recalled that it did not go through without opposition: 'Some persons came to me thinking I would help them protest this move ... I refused and Sun Yat-sen went firmly ahead ...' She remarked how far Sun had moved: 'When those in his own party refused to go along with him, he told them they must go the revolutionary way or get out. If they did not, he himself would join the Communist Party.'

Right in the middle of the Congress the news reached Canton that Lenin had died. The Congress suspended its sittings for three days. The following month a special memorial meeting attended by both Ching-ling and Sun was held in Canton to commemorate Lenin.

The reorganized party needed a military force capable of sustaining the new regime. A new Military Academy, at Whampoa, a suburb of Canton, was founded in May 1924. Chiang Kai-shek, recently returned from Moscow, was put at its head. Chou En-Lai became chief political commissar.

Sun could now begin to implement new social policies. Canton became known as 'Red Canton' and even 'the Moscow of the Far East'.

The main issue, the reunification of the country, however, still had to be tackled. This time, instead of launching a new Northern Expedition, Sun himself was invited to Peking by a new regime there. He set off by boat with Ching-ling in November 1924 on what was to be his last journey. They travelled via Japan, where Ching-ling delivered one of her major addresses, at Nagasaki, on the emancipation of women. In the meantime, 'the wives and daughters of Tientsin' were drafting a moving appeal for Ching-ling to be present at the upcoming conference the Suns were due to attend in Peking. Ching-ling's voice was audible in this appeal.

Let [women's] legal, financial and 'educational' situation be equal to that of men. Let daughters inherit as well as sons. Let the old educational system which produced 'good wives and tender mothers' (Confucius) be abolished and one created which turns girls into real human beings. Let very severe penalties be imposed upon those who drown little girls, who mistreat their wives or daughters-in-law, who bind their daughters' feet or pierce their ears . . . Let the enslavement of girls, concubinage, the practice of raising a fiancée along with her future husband, and prostitution be abolished. Let the patriarchal family system be replaced by that of the 'small family', each married couple constituting a separate household. Let the ridiculous honours formerly given to chaste women – including commemorative arches, etc. – be abolished. Let a man who is contemplating marriage with a young woman or with a widow first be able to enter into a social relationship with her which will allow him to get to know her. Let the right to divorce be granted to women who are unhappy in their marriages. Let the freedom of young women who do not want to marry be respected.

Ching-ling reached Tientsin on 4 December, with Sun already a very sick man. It was on this occasion that Mme Chou En-lai saw her, and recorded her impression in her funeral valedictory. On 27 January 1925, before any of the planned negotiations could take place, Sun entered hospital in Peking. He died on 12 March 1925, of cancer of the liver, aged fifty-eight. Ching-ling was with him at his death-bed.

On his death-bed Sun made it clearer than ever in what direction he wanted China to go. He dictated two documents the day before he died. One was his Political Testament, in which he called on his followers to hold fast to the new radical policies of the Kuomintang. The other was a Letter to the Soviet Union, in which he reiterated: 'I have instructed the party to remain in constant contact with you.' Finally, he added to his Political Testament a codicil which stated simply: 'Because I have been entirely absorbed by public affairs, I have not taken care of my personal fortune. I leave what I possess, my books, my house and anything else I own to my wife, Soong Ching-ling.'

In spite of his acute suffering, Sun managed to do all the crucial things just before he died. His last words were: 'Peace, struggle, save China ...'

Millions of dollars and other currencies had passed through

1912 With a classmate at school in Macon, Georgia, USA

1923   On board the first aeroplane built in China, named 'Rosamonde' after Ching-ling's Christian name

1923   With Sun Yat-sen on board a warship on the first anniversary of the escape from Canton. Sun is wearing the high-collared suit he designed and pioneered – known in China as the 'Sun Yat-sen suit' and by the rest of the world as the 'Mao suit'

December 1924   Ching-ling and Sun at Tientsin, three months before Sun's death

January 1926 Ching-ling, then head of the Women's Department of the Kuomintang, with representatives of women's organizations at Canton

September 1927 Crowds greet Ching-ling on arrival in Moscow at the start of her exile

Right: A very 'European' Ching-ling in exile in Europe

Below: February 1933 After lunch at Ching-ling's house in Shanghai. From the left: Agnes Smedley, George Bernard Shaw, Ching-ling, Ts'ai Yuan-p'ei (front), Harold Isaacs (partly obscured), Lin Yu-tang, Lu Hsun

Wartime Chungking   The three Soong sisters together

1942   A reserved Ching-ling with her two sisters and Chiang Kai-shek in Chungking. Ching-ling gave this picture to Helen Snow and inscribed on the back 'UF' (United Front)

1956 Ching-ling
on an inspection
tour in a minority
area on the
southern border

November 1957
Ching-ling,
the only non-
Communist
representative at the
meeting of world
Communist parties
in Moscow, watches
Mao sign the final
declaration

Left: 1960 With
Mme Chou En-lai
(centre) and Tsai
Chang, President of
the All-China
Women's Federation
Below: 1981 Deng
Xiaoping, Li
Hsien-nien (now
President) and
Mme Chou En-lai
pay their
last respects to
Ching-ling

his hands, yet he died with almost nothing. The only thing of substance he left to Ching-ling was the house in rue Molière. Even this, according to his bodyguard, Cohen, was heavily mortgaged.

Against some opposition Ching-ling insisted on a Christian funeral service, out of deference to Sun's beliefs and wishes. She chose the hymns herself: 'Jesu, Lover of My Soul', 'Crossing the Bar' and 'Wonderful Words of Life'. When Sun's embalmed body was transferred to a pavilion in Peking's Central Park, more than 100,000 people accompanied it, turning the occasion into a huge mass demonstration. It took well over a week for the crowds, estimated at half a million people, to file past his coffin when it was displayed in Central Park.

This vast outpouring of grief was also a manifestation of political support for Sun's ideals and for the person who had inherited the mantle of those ideals, Ching-ling.

CHAPTER THREE

Towards Exile: 1925–31

There were many people who thought, and hoped, that Ching-ling would fade into the background on the death of Sun. In a more difficult situation than that in Russia, she rapidly came to play a much more prominent role than did Lenin's widow, Krupskaya. She managed to fuse two very demanding roles – keeper of the flame for Sun's ideals and coming into her own as a national figure, with a unique moral authority which she retained through the dark days ahead. She did this in spite of the heavy odds stacked against her, first of all as a woman in a male-dominated movement, in a patriarchal and Confucian society. Ching-ling was basically a private and shy person but she turned herself into a good orator and steeled herself to become a public figure.

Ching-ling's first major act after Sun's death was to condemn the British shooting of unarmed Chinese civilians in Shanghai on 30 May 1925 (the 'May the 30th Incident'), which started from a demonstration protesting about the killing of a Chinese worker by a Japanese. This incident was one of many such which deepened Ching-ling's anger with the Western powers. And it also triggered broad national resentment.

In June 1925 a total strike broke out in Britain's colony of Hong Kong, which lasted nearly one and a half years and brought the colony to its knees. Hong Kong – 'Fragrant Harbour' – became Chou Kong – 'Stinking Harbour'. There was a highly charged atmosphere in Canton, which was a stone's throw from Hong Kong.

Ching-ling came from Shanghai for the Second Congress of the Kuomintang in January 1926. A young Russian interpreter, Vera Vishnyakova, recalled that 'an enormous crowd led by representatives of the government and public organization[s] went down to the pier to meet her'. Ching-ling was elected to the praesidium of the Congress, at which the left and centre-left won an outright majority in the key bodies. Some right-wing Kuomintang officials were expelled.

But the right was not going to lie down. They chose as their man Chiang Kai-shek – who had himself decided to ally with the forces of the right rather than the left.

He then showed his ability to employ unpredictable and fluid tactics. He organized an attack on the Soviet advisers in Canton and on the Chinese Communists there – and then apologized, saying the whole thing had been due to a misunderstanding. By May 1926 the Communists had been forced out of the leadership of the department of organization and propaganda. In a politically astute move, Chiang began to woo Ching-ling's younger sister, Mei-ling. Ching-ling energetically opposed the idea of a liaison. She said that she would rather die than see her sister marry that disreputable man.

Chiang then launched a Northern Expedition, which

headed for the strategic centre of China, the triple city of Wuhan on the Yangtse, consisting of Hankow, Wuchang and Hanyang (Chiang himself made only a fleeting visit to Wuhan). Owing to the Western powers' interference, it was not possible to get to Wuhan by sea and river, so the members of the government had to make an extremely arduous 2,000-mile journey overland.

Ching-ling went in the first group, together with Sun Fo (Sun Yat-sen's son), Foreign Minister Eugene Chen, her brother T. V. Soong, Borodin, several Soviet advisers and bodyguards. The journey involved travelling by train, then junk, long stretches by sedan chair, more junks, sampans and finally train, sleeping wherever they could along the way. Some of the trip had to be made on foot, slogging through mud, and up and down mountains.

Wuhan welcomed the group excitedly. One of its three cities, Wuchang, was where the 1911 revolution had started, and was thus a place with a strong emotional bond for Ching-ling and the Kuomintang.

In Wuhan a new committee was formed in December 1926 to run the government. For the first time Ching-ling was assigned a prominent administrative post. Some have said that she was not really a central leader. But she was. Although she did not have great leadership ability in the conventional sense of the word, she exercised leadership through the force of her personality, and because of her moral and almost emotional prestige. Along with Eugene Chen and General Teng Yen-ta she represented the left wing of the Kuomintang during the Wuhan period.

She divided her time between work in the government as

such and women's affairs. One of her major achievements was the setting up of the Women's Political Training School at the beginning of 1927. She gave a number of talks there, including 'Women Should Join the National Revolution' and 'On Women's Liberation in China'. In the first of these, among the points she made was that women 'should be against women oppressing women' and she insisted on the fundamental principle of men and women being treated equally – by each other as well as by the opposite sex. In the second talk she argued that women should not be treated as 'a sex', but as persons and that women should not make it their main goal to fight for separate women's goals – because these (equality, etc.) would automatically be achieved with 'the revolution'.

Although the Wuhan government was precarious, its fame spread around the world. Delegations came from all over the globe. Journalists like Randall Gould of the *Nation*, Vincent Sheean and Anna Louise Strong set their sights on seeing it in action – and meeting the fabulous Mme Sun Yat-sen.

One cannot but be struck by the warmth and admiration of the descriptions of Ching-ling. Randall Gould wrote: 'Most appealing of all those in [Wuhan] was Mme Sun, beautiful and shy, yet driven by tremendous inner fires. Everyone who knew her loved and deeply respected her.' Anna Louise Strong stayed with Ching-ling: 'Though in manner courteous almost to softness, she has in her a vein of iron. I saw her hold firmly to her path through every possible family and social pressure.' Strong also describes a social event which shows Ching-ling's grace, tact – and political savvy – under extreme pressure:

fractious guests, gunboats lurking just off the edge of the lawn:

I remember the garden party which she gave to raise money for the Nationalist Red Cross. It was the first social event in revolutionary Hankow attended by the representatives of foreign governments. Mrs Sun sensed keenly the latent social frictions ... Outside, on the river, were more than a score of gun-boats, ready at a moment's notice to fire on the city. Inside the garden, the representatives of those gun-boats were eating ice-cream and drinking soda-pop with Nationalist officials on behalf of wounded soldiers whom they regarded chiefly as enemies. Over it all presided Mrs Sun Yat-Sen, aware of every social friction, yet by the charm of her personality wringing aid even from the enemies and postponing inevitable collisions, that she might gain a breathing space for the northern advance of the revolutionary armies.

Most evocative of all is the portrait given by Vincent Sheean.

The door at the end of the darkened reception room on the second floor of the Ministry of Finance opened, and in came a small, shy Chinese lady in a black silk dress. In one of her delicate, nervous hands she held a lace handkerchief ... When she spoke her voice almost made me jump: it was so soft, so gentle, so unexpectedly sweet. The shutters had been closed to keep out the heat, and I could not see her until she had come quite near me. Then, looking down in bewilderment, I wondered who on earth she could be. Did Mme Sun Yat-sen have a daughter of whom I had never heard? It did not occur to me that this exquisite apparition, so fragile and timorous, could be the lady herself, the most celebrated woman revolutionary in the world ... I had certainly expected to meet something formidable. And instead, here I was face to face with a child-like figure of the most enchanting delicacy ... The events of the following months, the massacre of the Communists, the crushing of the labour movement in blood, were to arouse her indignation to such a pitch that she seemed, before one's eyes, to take on stature. Without physical or intellectual power, by sheer force of character, purity of motive, sovereign honesty, she became heroic. In the wreck of the Chinese Revolution this phenomenon was one of the most extraordinary: generals and orators fell to pieces, yielded, fled, or were silent, but the one revolutionary who could not be crushed and would not be still was the fragile little widow of Sun Yat-sen.

Events were conspiring against the Wuhan experiment. In January 1927 the people of Wuhan had seized the British concessions there. Percy Chen, the son of Foreign Minister Eugene Chen, recalls that Ching-ling spoke up in favour of not returning the concessions. Her brother, T. V. Soong, was neutral. Borodin argued that they should avoid conflict with the imperialist powers for the time being. In the end the British had to abandon their concession – the first successful takeover by China of imperialist possessions.

This signal success set off repercussions all over China (and in the Western world). The coalition of Western powers and Chinese conservatives and gangsters intrigued to bring down the Wuhan group and destroy the Chinese left. A strong trend began to emerge in Wuhan to abandon the government's radical policies and compromise with the Kuomintang right.

On 12 April 1927 Chiang Kai-shek, who had stayed away from Wuhan, and had tried to detain members of the government (with success in some cases) at Nanchang en route north, moved against the Communists in Shanghai. A massacre was carried out, co-ordinated with the Green Gang, the main underground organization which provided many of the

killers, and the foreign business community. Thousands of
Communists were slaughtered in the most gruesome manner;
many were tortured. Women were disembowelled and strangled with their own entrails. Sheean records being with
Ching-ling a few weeks later when a similar threat weighed
over Wuhan. They were with the young American radical
Rayna Prohme, who was a close friend of them both, and a
potential target for retribution.

Suddenly, the conversation took a gruesome turn. It would have
been gruesome under any conditions, but on that particular day,
in the presence of two women who stood in such awful peril, it
made my blood run cold. Mme Sun began it by speaking of the
tortures to which the twenty Communists (including little Phyllis
Li, the daughter of Li Ta-chao) had been subjected in Peking. She
explained the difference between garrotting and plain strangling,
named a number of the more agonizing torments in use among the
Chinese reactionaries, and discussed the relative merits of the
various forms of execution from the point of view of the person to
be executed. Although she seemed a little nervous, and was conscious that the dangers she discussed were only a few hours away,
I do not believe she was primarily thinking of herself; she was
indirectly attempting to persuade Rayna Prohme to go to the
American Consulate for the night.

The massacre virtually wiped out the Communists in their
urban stronghold, Shanghai. Of the key leaders, only Chou
En-lai escaped. Ching-ling and her colleagues in the Central
Executive Committee issued a statement condemning
Chiang's action. This was also signed by the young Communist leader Mao Tse-tung (still a member of the Kuomintang)
and other Communist figures. Chiang and his partisans were

officially expelled from the Kuomintang. On 18 April Chiang
and his group set up a rival 'national government' at Nanking,
claiming to be the legitimate heirs of Sun Yat-sen. For the
next few months a tussle went on, with the two governments
both claiming legitimacy. A tendency emerged among many
at Wuhan to compromise with Chiang.

Ching-ling led the fight against a compromise, and in this
she had the support of Eugene Chen and Teng Yen-ta. But
Sun Yat-sen's son, Sun Fo, was less resolute – as was the
Soviet regime, which continued to urge compromise. One of
the only voices audible from Moscow condemning Chiang's
massacre was that of his eldest son, Chiang Ching-kuo, who
landed himself in trouble (including prison) by taking a line
which clashed with that of Stalin and basically coincided
with that of Trotsky.

In the meantime Ching-ling was doing all she could, not
merely to stiffen the backbone of the regime but also to give
assistance to the troops wounded in the continuing fighting
in the Northern Expedition.

The final split between the left and the right was not long
coming. Anticipating it, Ching-ling denounced the right on
14 July 1927:

I feel that it is necessary at this time to explain as a member of
the Central Executive Committee of the Kuomintang, that we have
reached a point where definition is necessary, and where some
members of the party executive are so defining the principles and
policies of Sun Yat-sen, that they seem to me to do violence to Sun's
ideas and ideals. Feeling thus, I must disassociate myself from active
participation in the carrying out of these new policies of the party.
    . . . At the moment, I feel that we are turning aside from Sun Yat-

sen's policy of leading and strengthening the people. Therefore I must withdraw until wiser policies prevail.

There is no despair in my heart for the revolution. My disheartenment is only for the path into which some of those who had been leading the revolution have strayed.

Because of the prestige attaching to her name, her voice itself carried power – in particular, because this voice carried the authority of Sun Yat-sen. This statement was printed in the local newspaper, the Hankow *People's Tribune*. The paper was promptly suppressed. The very next day the head of the Wuhan government, the ineffectual Wang Ching-wei, announced the expulsion of the Communists from the Kuomintang and made his peace with Nanking. The Soviet advisers were expelled and the remaining Communists went underground.

Mme Sun suggested that revolutionary forces in the government should go to Canton and entrench there. But the other leaders wavered. Only some Communists made off south with their troops in time. Borodin paid Ching-ling the ultimate, if quaintly sexist, compliment when he called her 'the only man in the whole left wing of the Kuomintang'.

The emotion of the time was captured by the Russian interpreter, Vishnyakova:

The Wuhan period is the most complex and contradictory in the history of the Chinese revolution of 1925–1927, a time of great victories and crushing defeats, heroic deeds and fatal errors. I remember how feverishly the pulse of Wuhan's political life beat ... events ... flashed by, one after the other, like woodchips in a whirlpool. Time was compressed to the limits.

The left had to get out of Wuhan – fast. An agent of Chiang Kai-shek, a former left-winger whose shift was not known to the Wuhan radicals, tried to persuade Borodin it was safe to travel back via Shanghai. But Ching-ling was in the room and she was the one who said it was a trap. She herself had to get out, too. She travelled in secret down the Yangtse, spending the entire five-day journey hidden below decks in the sweltering heat of midsummer.

On 1 August some Communist forces which had escaped from Hankow launched an uprising at Nanchang against the Kuomintang – in effect, the founding of what was to become the Communist army and the beginning of the armed struggle to defeat the Kuomintang. On the same day a declaration was issued denouncing the betrayal by Chiang Kai-shek and Wang Ching-wei: it bore the signature of Ching-ling, as well as that of Mao and other leading figures. In lending her name to this declaration, Ching-ling gave her open support to the attempt to overthrow Chiang by force.

But it was very hard for Ching-ling, even with her prominence, to make her voice heard. She had to preserve her independence and find somewhere where she could be safe. Paradoxically, this place was Moscow. Borodin had envisaged such a possibility and had asked Vishnyakova to start giving Ching-ling Russian lessons – though in the end there was no time to do so. Apart from Moscow being a safe haven, the mere fact of Ching-ling going there would be a powerful statement in its own right.

To get there she had to make a long and hazardous journey. First, from Hankow down the Yangtse to Shanghai. There she had to make sure that she was neither murdered (as her brother, T. V. Soong, told her she might be), nor incarcerated and kept incommunicado. At the end of August Ching-ling and her American friend, Rayna Prohme, made their way down to the river in the middle of the night. They were rowed by sampan to a Soviet steamer that sailed at dawn. A young Communist who was being sent clandestinely to Russia for military training was on the same boat. His description of the mood of those on the boat catches the relief, and the exultation, of those escaping from a nightmare. But this, too, was a dream, soon to be shattered by the harsh reality of Stalin's Russia. As the ship sailed out of Shanghai harbour:

We crawled out from the hold and onto the deck. It was like being born again. The early autumn sun lifted our spirits, and we began to dance for joy and to sing the Internationale. We sailed further and further out to sea, gradually losing sight of the shores of the motherland. The water was like glass and our mood changed to one of meditation. We leant against the railings and gazed pensively into the distance, while thoughts flooded in. As individuals we were each beginning a new chapter in our lives, and it seemed to us as if the Chinese Revolution was also beginning a new chapter in which each word and each letter would be written in bullets and blood.

When the ship docked at Vladivostok, Ching-ling and her companions were met by a special train which took them to Moscow. On the long journey across Siberia crowds greeted Ching-ling at every stop. Very early one morning Yolanda Chen, one of the daughters of the Kuomintang Foreign Minister, got up and went to the window of the train and was hailed by a large crowd at a small Siberian station, who mistook her for Mme Sun.

At Moscow Ching-ling was met by Maxim Litvinov, soon

to be Soviet Foreign Minister. She and the others were put up in the Hotel Metropole in central Moscow. Apart from Litvinov, Ching-ling also met Mikhail Kalinin, the President of the USSR, and his wife, who became good friends, and Alexandra Kollontai. She left shortly afterwards for a holiday in the Caucasus.

It was the worst possible time to be in the Soviet Union. The Chinese Revolution was one of the three key issues in the imminent rupture between Stalin and Trotsky. Stalin had misread the situation in China badly, and was on the look-out for scapegoats and this meant anyone who had been in China, or was connected with the Chinese Revolution. Borodin, who reached Moscow soon after Ching-ling, having made an incredibly dangerous drive across the Gobi desert, was muzzled and shunted into a minor post.

Things came to a head in November. On the tenth anniversary of the Bolshevik Revolution, Ching-ling was invited to Red Square to watch the parade. She stood with the Soviet leaders on the old, original wooden mausoleum for Lenin. Eugene Chen's son Percy recalls the scene.

It was snowing and extremely cold. We had not learned the trick of taking newspapers with us to put under our feet to stand on, so our feet were frozen and very painful. I wore shoes with rubber soles, which to a certain extent insulated me from the cold. But my father and Madame Sun suffered since they were wearing thin-soled leather shoes inside rubber overshoes ...

On our way back from Red Square to the Metropole Hotel we ... saw crowds gathered around some speakers. We then saw the police surge from a side alley and begin to disperse the crowds. They arrested some of the speakers and took them away.

In fact, this was the last attempt by Trotsky and his colleagues to appeal to the people. A few weeks later the former Soviet emissary in China, Joffe, who was close to Trotsky and the Chinese *émigrés*, committed suicide.

Ching-ling was now politically isolated in Moscow, except for her friends from China. Teng Yen-ta had been forced to flee Russia after being injudiciously frank at a meeting of the Communist International. There was little solace from Stalin. Ching-ling and Eugene Chen went to see him: Stalin urged them to go back to China and co-operate with Chiang Kai-shek. The only bright spot seems to have been Ching-ling's friendship with the Kalinins, with whom she enjoyed going sleigh-riding at their house at Arkhangelskoye, outside Moscow.

Ching-ling was miserable, and low on funds. One evening she went with Sheean and others to the Bolshoi to see a performance of a new ballet called *The Red Poppy*, about the Chinese Revolution. They sat in a grand box. But the production was crude and insensitive. Sheean also recalls going to the cinema with Rayna Prohme and Ching-ling to see the newsreel films of her arrival in Moscow.

The expedition made her nervous, for she had a dread of being recognized in the streets. The Foreign Office had given her a motorcar for the length of her stay, and she used to pull down all the blinds the moment she got into it, so as to move about Moscow as invisibly as possible. We reached the cinema in this darkened car, and when it had drawn up at the curb Rayna stood guard over it while I got the tickets. Then, the way being clear, Mme Sun made her dash from the car to the darkened interior of the theatre ... Mme Sun was getting more and more nervous, and her appearance had already been noticed by two or three of the people sitting near us.

Eventually the news films began, and the first of them was the arrival of Soong Ching-ling in Moscow.

It did not last long – six or seven minutes, perhaps – but during that time Mme Sun tore one of her minute handkerchiefs into bits.

When it [the train] had come to a stop the camera moved nearer, and we saw the small figure of Mme Sun, hesitant and bewildered, appear on the steps to be greeted by Litvinov. At this Mme Sun, sitting beside me, gasped and whispered that she could not stand it any more.

Mme Sun was born fragile, with a nervous disposition. In Russia she had several breakdowns. All her life her health followed the cycles of political events. But she always lived beyond her strength. She steeled herself to be a revolutionary and her will was never broken. Nor did she become a neurotic. She always kept her serenity. How hard this was for her at first her close friend Vincent Sheean touchingly described:

The painful shyness from which Mme Sun suffered was not unknown to me; I had seen it in English people, for instance, particularly among artists or writers; but she was the only person so afflicted who ever, in my experience, deliberately faced it out. When she felt it her duty to do something that involved a public appearance she did it, although the agony was such that she might be obliged to take to her bed for days afterwards. In Moscow she tore all her handkerchiefs to ribbons and had to get new ones. Public attention was such torture to her that for this reason alone I never believed she was or could become an active revolutionary leader. In the hurly-burly passions of a street insurrection she would have been like a white rose in a furnace.

Personal tragedy struck again. A rumour began to spread that she had run away to Moscow with Eugene Chen. Other false reports linked her to both Teng Yen-ta and Mikhail Borodin (who was known as something of a ladies' man). These rumours hurt Ching-ling deeply as in China at the time marrying any 'scandal' would diminish her appeal, particularly as Mme Sun, which was important in campaigning for her ideals.

Because she could not remarry, and because of the turmoil surrounding her, friendships became very important to her. The person who seemed to be closest to her at this time was the vivacious young American radical Rayna Prohme, who had escaped with her from Shanghai. Ching-ling was a person who liked to lavish affection on her friends, and right in the middle of the upheavals at Wuhan she had designed a dress for Rayna. In Russia Ching-ling fell out with her. While Ching-ling was in the Caucasus, Rayna heard about the rumour linking Eugene Chen and Ching-ling and, to avoid hurting Ching-ling, kept this from her when she got back to Moscow. Ching-ling was extremely upset; she thought this was too important for her not to know. She had a breakdown. Sadly, the misunderstanding was resolved only just before Rayna Prohme's sudden death. Her death, which anyway would have been a shattering blow to Ching-ling, was doubly so, because Ching-ling had had only a few days to make up with her closest friend.

On her death-bed Rayna Prohme wore the dress Ching-ling had given her.

The funeral took place on a bitterly cold Russian winter day, as Sheean described:

... as I walked along I became conscious of the shivering, bent figure of Mme Sun Yat-sen. Her income had been cut off from China; she was too proud to accept the help of strangers; she had no winter clothing at all, and was walking through the dreary, frozen streets in a thin dark cloak. The motorcar loaned to her by the Soviet Foreign Office followed behind the procession; it was at least warm. I tried to persuade her to get into it, but she would not. She walked every step of the way across the city, her lovely face bent down towards her folded arms. She had recovered from her own illness only a few days before, and her pallor was extreme. Even through the cold haze in which everything moved on that day I was aware that Soong Ching-ling was now the loneliest of exiles, shivering through the early dark behind the bier of her most disinterested friend.

The night of the funeral Borodin came to see Sheean:

He had come to say good-bye, he said, and to explain why he had not gone to the funeral. On principle he never went to funerals. The mind must be kept resolutely on its purposes.

His voice was deeply moved, and he controlled it with difficulty.

He did not look at me, but walked from the window to the door and back again.

'I know what this is,' he said. 'I know exactly. But what is needed is the long view. I have come here to ask you to take the long view – China, Russia ... A wonderful friend and a wonderful revolutionary instrument have disappeared together. But there is no use in anything unless we take the long view. Remember that. China, Russia ...'

After a while he shook hands and went away.

Almost simultaneously came bitter personal news from China: Ching-ling's sister Mei-ling was to marry Chiang Kai-shek. According to Edgar Snow, Chiang had already proposed to Ching-ling after the death of Sun. Ching-ling, according to Snow, 'thought it was politics, not love, and declined'.

Some years later Snow talked to Ching-ling about her sister's marriage. 'I understand your mother made him promise to study the Bible before she consented to the marriage?'

'That's true,' said Ching-ling. 'He would have agreed to be a Holy Roller to marry Mei-ling. He needed her to build a dynasty.'

Ching-ling asked Eugene Chen to send Mei-ling a telegram urging her not to marry 'that Bluebeard'.

Ching-ling never forgave her sister for lending the Soong name to Chiang. The marriage was particularly bitter since it meant her family was deliberately choosing to make a break with Ching-ling and to give Chiang Kai-shek cover to appropriate the legacy of Sun Yat-sen.

The wedding was a grandiose and well-publicized affair, which was conducted beneath a portrait of Sun Yat-sen, under which Chiang and Mei-ling had themselves conspicuously posed for the wedding photographs.

This marked the political break between Ching-ling and her family. Henceforth they followed different paths. Mei-ling became the main link between the Kuomintang government and America. She was the first woman to address the US Congress and she swept America off its feet. For years she was named one of the ten most popular women in the world (by the Americans). Ai-ling, in contrast, led the life of a recluse. She was reportedly the shrewdest and most unscrupulous woman entrepreneur in the world at a time when few women were directly involved in business. She concentrated on accumulating a vast fortune – though, unlike Mei-ling, she hid it rather than flaunted it. Ching-ling's brother, T. V. Soong, who was successively Kuomintang Finance Minister, Foreign Minister and Premier, was widely thought to be the richest man in the world.

The Soongs, who had by then formed a powerful camarilla with the Kungs, the family of Ai-ling's husband, now had the military and political backing of Chiang Kai-shek. Together, they dominated Chinese politics in an increasingly rightward direction. Although the whole dynasty was built on Ching-ling's marriage, she devoted her life to the long and arduous task of bringing that dynasty down. Hereafter, in spite of the close personal feelings involved, the conflict was tragically irreconcilable in China's bitterly polarized politics.

Soon after his wedding Chiang broke off all relations with Russia. Soviet diplomats in Canton were executed after the ill-fated Canton Uprising of 11 December ('the Canton Commune'), which was suppressed with what was in the Chinese context average brutality. Ching-ling telegraphed Chiang:

I was just about to come back to China when I heard that you had proposed breaking diplomatic relations with Russia and expelling the Russian advisers. This would be suicidal and would leave our party and our country isolated – and you will go down in history as a criminal who has ruined our party and the country ... [If you do not] reconsider ... I shall have no choice but to stay here rather longer, to show that I am opposed to your unjust and suicidal policies.

Meanwhile, she tried to stake out a terrain on which to make her views heard. She accepted a position as a member of the praesidium of the League to Struggle against Imperialism and Colonial Oppression and travelled to Brussels in December 1927 for an important meeting of the League, at which she was elected Honorary President. Among her colleagues on the praesidium were Albert Einstein, Henri Barbusse, Jawaharlal Nehru, Upton Sinclair, Maxim Gorky, George Lansbury of the British Labour Party and Romain Rolland, who said of her later: 'Do you think that our brilliant ... Soong Ching-ling is only a beautiful flower whose fragrance can be felt around the world? No! No! She is really a lion who tries to break all nets.'

From Brussels she went to Berlin, where she had close friends. An American diplomat there reported to his government: 'Her half-year stay in Moscow has disillusioned her completely as to bolshevism and bolshevik propaganda in China.' But this may itself be American propaganda. Anyway, it fails to get to the roots of the nature of Ching-ling's commitment, or to differentiate between what may well have been her views about the immediate situation in Russia in 1927–8 and her overall view of the Chinese revolution and the need for keeping links with Russia. Her attitude was surely more like Borodin's: take the long view.

In May 1929 Ching-ling went back to China for Sun's official burial. Sun had asked to be buried at Nanking, where he had first been made President in 1912. The question of where and how to bury him was of the highest importance, and Chiang made sure he did not lose the chance to turn it into a political football.

Ching-ling had gone to the site in March 1926 for the ceremony of laying the foundation stone for the memorial building, which was to be a gigantic edifice embodying symbolic elements relating to Sun's political philosophy. The mausoleum was also a symbol of Confucian tradition, according to which the widow of the dead man was supposed to live in mourning by his tomb. Agnes Smedley visited the site with Chiang's closest aide:

Before leaving, Colonel Hwang took me through a small cottage still under construction.

'This house,' he explained, 'is being built for Madame Sun Yat-sen, the widow of the late Dr Sun. She will live here near the tomb.'

'Do you think Madame Sun will live here?' I asked.

'Oh, certainly! She is a member of the Central Committee of the party!'

'I thought she was in exile.'

His manner and voice became offensively sarcastic. He asked if she was in Moscow – and where was Borodin?

Chiang sent Ching-ling's younger brother Tse-liang to Berlin. Ching-ling agreed to come for the ceremony, but made her conditions clear:

I am proceeding to China for the purpose of attending to the removal of the remains of Dr Sun Yat-sen to the Purple Mountain where he desired to be buried.

In order to avoid any possible misunderstanding, I have to state that I emphatically adhere to my declaration made in Hankow on July 14th, 1927 ... my attendance at the burial is not to be interpreted as in any sense implying a modification or reversal of my decision to abstain from any direct or indirect work of the Kuomintang so long as its leadership is opposed to the fundamental policies of Dr Sun ...

Ching-ling travelled back on the Trans-Siberian railway in May 1929 and was met at Harbin by Kuomintang officials. She refused to have anything to do with her family, and stayed away from them even on the special train to Nanking. The ceremony took place on a sweltering muggy day in June. Chiang made sure it was on a grandiose scale. Ching-ling walked up the hundreds of steps to the mausoleum in a separate procession from her family and the Kuomintang leaders. She had insisted on this, which was a very demonstrative act in the Chinese style.

Then she went her way, back to Shanghai. She had pulled off the near-impossible: she had paid her respects to Sun; she had staked her claim to his legacy in the eyes of the people; yet she had demonstrated her refusal to co-operate with Chiang.

She was not going to be silent. On 1 August she sent a blistering telegram to the Anti-Imperialist League in Berlin:

While the oppressed nationalities today form a solid front against imperialist war and militarism, the reactionary Nanking Government is combining forces with the Imperialists in brutal repressions against the Chinese masses. Never has the treacherous character of the counter-revolutionary Kuomintang leaders been so shamelessly exposed to the world as today . . .

This blast from the heartland of Chiang's fief probably brought her as close to death as she had been since her escape from Canton. Powerful emissaries were sent to berate her – and threaten. Among them was the former secretary to Sun and ex-leftist, Tai Ch'i-tao. The encounter ended with this exchange:

Tai: 'I hope that you will not make any more statements, Mrs Sun.'

Soong: 'There is only one way to silence me, Mr Tai. Shoot me or imprison me. If you don't then it simply means that you admit you are not wrongly accused. But whatever you do, do it openly like me, don't . . . surround me with spies.'

Tai: 'I shall call again upon my return from Nanking.'

Soong: 'Further conversations would be useless – the gulf between us is too wide.'

As Tai left, he said: 'If you were anyone but Madame Sun, we would cut your head off.'

Ching-ling smiled. 'If you were the revolutionaries you pretend to be, you'd cut it off anyway.'

One of her oldest friends commented about her: 'She knew danger – and its limits.'

Early in 1930 Ching-ling went to Europe and again met Teng Yen-ta in Berlin. For Teng and her, as for all the *émigrés*, the place they wanted to be was back in their homeland, even at the cost of great personal danger. Teng went back and, after about one year in Europe, Ching-ling, too, returned to the rue Molière to take on Chiang as best she could at close quarters.

CHAPTER FOUR

Shanghai under Chiang: 1931–7

Ching-ling's return to Shanghai in June 1931 was a bitter one. Her sister was married to the man whom she felt had betrayed Sun Yat-sen's legacy and was now dominating Chinese politics. Opposition to the Kuomintang had been driven largely underground in the cities. And within weeks of Ching-ling's return her mother died, on 23 July 1931.

But Ching-ling had returned to China for one purpose – to carry on the struggle for a Chinese revolution. The only major organized force which had the same goal was the Communist Party, then operating mainly in remote rural areas. Her work throughout the 1930s (until the agreement to form a united Communist–Kuomintang front against Japan in 1937) was geared towards opposing both Japanese encroachment on China and the Kuomintang's policy of 'non-resistance', as well as its repression of internal dissent.

Ching-ling's strategy was always to devote herself to the great national issues ('save China', in effect), while at the same time focusing effort on several specific projects in the field of human rights and welfare assistance (e.g. for troops). Her significance lay not so much in the actual practical effect of what she achieved, though this was often important, as in her general and 'moral' appeal. Thus, for example, she was able to bring some real help to some political prisoners – and to be seen to be doing so – but she was unable to affect Chiang's policies as such. In a sense, although she was under constant surveillance, and was circumscribed in her actions, she could also operate with some freedom because she was not a political threat to the regime.

On 18 September 1931 Japan attacked the major city of Mukden (now Shenyang) in north-east China, marking the start of an all-out drive to take over first north-east China (Manchuria), which it turned into the puppet state of Manchukuo, and later most of coastal and riverine China. The Japanese attack was a watershed in terms of political attitudes and decisions. Both Communists and non-Communists (including Mme Sun) called immediately and decisively for all-out resistance to the Japanese. Chiang adopted a policy of non-resistance; he wanted to save his energies for fighting the Communists.

Not everyone in the Kuomintang, however, saw things the same way. In January 1932 the Japanese attacked Shanghai, and bombed it heavily from the air. The Kuomintang 19th Route Army put up courageous resistance, with tremendous popular support. Demonstrations took place in Peking and elsewhere strongly supporting a policy of resisting the Japanese. From this point on the tide of organized popular opinion can be said to have turned against the Kuomintang, which was seen as derelict in the face of Japan's aggression. Ching-ling went into action immediately to organize relief work and medical care. She raised a large amount of money and set up a 300-bed hospital for wounded soldiers.

Meanwhile, though, if Chiang was inactive against the Japanese, who were trying to dismember China, he was not inactive against his domestic opponents. And the fight to protect political prisoners and defend civil rights became Ching-ling's main concern. Not long after he returned to China, Teng Yen-ta, who had come back to try to revive a genuine left Kuomintang, was arrested. According to Agnes Smedley, Ching-ling broke her own vow never to ask a favour of her brother-in-law; he let her plead for Teng and when she had finished told her he had been killed. Teng had reportedly been tortured for months and finally strangled with wire by an executioner whose speciality was to make the strangulation last as long as possible.

That this was a shattering and tragic blow, both personally and politically, comes through strongly from Ching-ling's anguished denunciation of the time, which proclaimed: 'The Kuomintang is no longer a political power.'

It is no longer possible to hide the fact that the Kuomintang as a political power has ceased to exist. It has been liquidated, not by its opponents outside the Party, but by its own leaders within the Party.

... faithful and true revolutionaries have been deliberately tortured to death in many cruel ways, the latest example being the murder of Teng Yen-ta.

... I, for one, cannot bear to witness the work of forty years by Sun Yat-sen being destroyed by a handful of self-seeking and scheming Kuomintang militarists and politicians. Still more unbearable is it for me to see the subjection of a nation of 475,000,000 to imperialism, brought about by the Kuomintang's betrayal of its own doctrine.

The following year there was the case which, according to Edgar Snow, saddened Ching-ling the most – the killing of six young Chinese writers. They 'were made to dig their own graves. Then they were bound, thrown into the pits and buried alive, an old Chinese punishment for subversives.' Shortly afterwards Snow discussed the killings with Ching-ling: 'That', said Ching-ling bitterly, 'is our Christian General-issimo – burying our best young people alive. Evidently in his Bible studies he has not reached the Corinthians.'

'You think he personally knew about it?' Snow asked.

'He is responsible for all the killings. He began it with the counter-revolution [of 1927]. That's why I'll never take a seat in any Kuomintang government as long as he is dictator. And that's why if he's a Christian I am not.'

Ching-ling moved to build an institutional network which could help to protect radicals. In late 1932 she set up an organization called the China League for Civil Rights, together with a group of eminent Chinese cultural figures, including the great writer Lu Hsun; although harassed and censored, he was virtually immune from personal assault because of his enormous reputation. Also involved was the former Kuomintang Education Minister, Ts'ai Yuan-p'ei, a very conservative but prestigious figure who had been revolted by the murder of Teng Yen-ta. A close colleague of Ts'ai, Yang Chien, an activist, was Secretary of the League. There were also two Americans involved: Agnes Smedley and Harold Isaacs, a young newspaper correspondent and editor of the magazine *China Forum*.

When the League was first set up Ching-ling spoke out vigorously:

There is another frightful evil against which the League for Civil Rights must wage an uncompromising war. That is the system of torture of political prisoners, a system unequalled in the world . . .

Helpless against this torture, helpless against the barbarity of their jailers, they depend on us outside to release them from lingering death.

Ching-ling and the League were not to be allowed to function unmolested, though she and Lu Hsun could not be attacked directly. A leading woman writer, Ting Ling, who was a close associate of Mme Sun's, was abducted. Ting Ling's husband had been one of the six young writers buried alive in 1931 about whom Ching-ling had talked to Edgar Snow. Gangsters then murdered the Secretary of the League, Yang Chien. Serious threats were made against other prominent members of the League, including the writer Lin Yu-tang. Leading members, including Lin, either were frightened off or drifted away. Isaacs recalls that 'Soong Ching-ling led this band a good deal further than many in it wanted to go . . .' Perhaps it should be said that she could go further than most – and did. But the League collapsed, all the same, under relentless pressure.

Alongside this activity at home Ching-ling was using her unique standing to try to get information about China to the outside world and arouse solidarity abroad. In February 1933 Ching-ling invited George Bernard Shaw to lunch at her home. Agnes Smedley reportedly remembered the occasion this way:

It was a very jovial and effective meeting. The occasion was filled with thought-provoking and witty remarks by Lu Xun [Hsun] and Bernard Shaw, two great humorists, and Soong Ching-Ling's laughter. But, as the situation outside was getting extremely tense, we were getting ready to be jailed by the Chinese fascists. A taste of Chinese fascism would give us more hard evidence for our fight against international fascism. Shaw said his Fabianism would probably collapse and he would become a revolutionary if he were tried by Chinese law and jailed in a feudal prison.

To some of the League members it seemed sad that Shaw would not go any further than to make witty remarks. As Isaacs recalled the event:

We hoped, vainly as it turned out, that we could get Shaw to denounce Kuomintang repression and make a worldwide propaganda score with whatever he might say about it. Unfortunately, and to our considerable chagrin, we found we never could keep the aging Shaw's attention focused long enough on the matters that interested us.

Ching-ling also wrote in the US magazine the *Nation* (whose China correspondent, Randall Gould, was a supporter of hers). When the World Committee Against Fascism was founded in Paris in 1933, Ching-ling was elected Vice-President (the French writer Henri Barbusse was President). Perhaps her most daring initiative was to convene a clandestine conference in Shanghai in September 1933 – the Far East Conference of the World Committee Against Imperialist War. Among the foreign delegates were a British peer, Lord Marley, who took the chair, and the editor of the French Communist Party daily, *L'Humanité*, Paul Vaillant-Couturier. Ching-ling delivered a stirring opening address, in which she roundly denounced Britain, France and the USA, as well as Japan, for threatening China. She also announced her explicit support for the Chinese Communists and their army.

She attracted foreign intellectuals and activists to her own work, recognizing the key role they could play, with both relative immunity and access to the outside world. Among those with whom she worked at the time were Edgar Snow, Rewi Alley, Dr George Hatem (Ma Haide), Agnes Smedley and Harold Isaacs. It was she who in 1936 arranged for Edgar Snow and Dr Hatem to get into the Communist areas and meet Mao – an enterprise immortalized in Snow's *Red Star Over China* (the participation of Dr Hatem, who stayed on, was kept secret at the time to protect his position and contacts in the Kuomintang-controlled areas). Also, little known is the fact that she was instrumental in saving Ho Chi Minh, who was in hiding in Shanghai in the years 1933–4, after a lucky escape from Hong Kong. Ho had been tremendously influenced by Sun Yat-sen, and Ching-ling had met him in Brussels in the late 1920s, together with Nehru.

Nor did she neglect events further afield. When the Nazis seized power in Germany in 1933, she, together with Lu Hsun, led a protest delegation to the German Consulate in Shanghai. And in May 1933 she issued a 'Denunciation of the Persecution of German Progressives and the Jewish People' which was not only a very principled statement, but also a very informed one, reflecting her intimate acquaintance with German culture and language, and the work of people like Thomas Mann, Lion Feuchtwanger and Kaethe Kollwitz.

All those who met Ching-ling during these difficult years in Shanghai were struck both by her commitment to fighting for a better China and by her serenity in the midst of relentless personal and political anguish. As Helen Snow (Nym Wales), who met her then, put it:

Until quite recently, her whole life had been a series of defeats, frustrations, assassinations of friends or their death from overwork and strain. It is a marvel that she survived with her sanity intact. Yet she never became callous to human suffering – which is the defense the Chinese have learned to build up over the centuries.

This was particularly remarkable, since the person she held mainly responsible for the suffering was her brother-in-law, with the connivance of her own sister – without whom, though, Ching-ling said, the excesses 'might have been much worse'. In her May 1933 article in the *Nation* she chose to make a point of picking out her brother T. V. Soong, of whom she was very fond. T. V., who at the time was Kuomintang Minister of Finance, was denounced by her in the article for his hypocritical stance on the question of resisting Japan.

Yet, in spite of all the things the Kuomintang had done, in which her family were implicated to varying degrees, Ching-ling remained emotionally close to them. Randall Gould, the *Nation* correspondent, recalled:

One afternoon in the early 1930s when I was waiting in Dr Sun's house in Rue Molière ... suddenly the door opened and in trooped the three sisters ... laughing and chattering like schoolgirls. This was at a period when Madame Sun was being watched by plain-clothes agents of the Nanking regime ... It was a time when the sound of her typewriter clacking away by night was reported to the Government as 'a secret radio set communicating with Moscow.' Yet here was Madame Sun bringing home, with every appearance of constant familiarity, the wives of two of the highest officials of the National Government against which she had set her face ...

One of the few people who caught a glimpse of Ching-ling's private life around this time was Edgar Snow:

Ching-ling liked beautiful things and chose the few external furnishings of her life with unerring taste. Her home was always immaculate, with an effect of warmth and simplicity. She had a few treasured paintings and scrolls and her rooms were usually bright with exotic flowers. She dressed in subdued colors in gowns of youthful style and she was always perfectly groomed, her jet hair caught severely back and ending in a bun, leaving her delicately boned features in fine cameo relief. Except for a jade hairpin or a clasp she seldom wore any ornament.

Ching-ling liked Western opera and had a fine collection of records. She liked to dance and occasionally gave parties for young people and thoroughly relaxed and enjoyed herself.

Snow also picked up on some of the qualities which were not obvious in public:

Coupled with [a] kind of toughness and independence in Ching-ling was an unexpected pixie quality which made her like to see pomp reduced to ridicule and to poke fun at anybody smug, complacent, chauvinistic or self-important. She was an accomplished mimic and loved to quote silly remarks by Chinese and foreign diplomats and politicians and their wives. When the benign Dr Kung, who had the same surname as Confucius (Kung Fu-tzu), announced that he was, in fact, the old gentleman's 'direct descendant,' Ching-ling henceforth referred to him as The Sage.

Ching-ling was also repelled by rich Chinese 'who felt no sense of shame at the degradation of "the people" and their ostentatious displays of wealth seemed to her vulgar insults to the nation'. She remarked to Edgar Snow about her sister

Ai-ling's financial wheeling and dealing: 'It's a pity she can't do it for the people instead of against them.'

Ching-ling described her own relationship with Sun Yat-sen as being based originally on hero worship. In fact, she seems to have inspired heroine worship of an almost miraculous kind in those who met her – both men and women. Isaacs and Sheean have left moving accounts of their devotion to her – and the sway she exercised over them. Edgar Snow called her 'the conscience and the constant heart of a "still unfinished revolution"'. But women were no less touched. When Helen Snow looked back years later, she wrote: 'I realize that Shanghai had only one golden-glamorous thing beyond compare. It was the brave and beautiful and lonely widow of Dr Sun Yat-sen.' And Anna Louise Strong wrote of her as 'the most gentle and exquisite creature I know anywhere in the world'.

While Ching-ling was fighting her battles in Shanghai, in the remote hinterland the Communists were changing the course of China's history. The Kuomintang launched a series of 'annihilation campaigns' against the Communists. In 1934, the main group of Communists in the rural base areas began the famous 'Long March' which was ultimately to bring a few thousand survivors (about five per cent of those who had started out) to safety in the remote area of Yenan, in Shensi Province in north-west China. The March, which lasted one year, covered some 6,000 miles, and involved crossing innumerable snow-covered mountains and wild grasslands, under constant attack from Kuomintang forces. One of the survivors was Deng Xiaoping.

The Long March gave the Communists not only a heroic image in the eyes of the nation, but also a fairly secure base, under united political leadership (which had been a problem prior to Mao's advent to undisputed primacy during the Long March). The Communist Party then based its appeal to the Chinese people on its call to resist Japanese aggression.

Japan had paused in 1933 after conquering the three north-eastern provinces, which they turned into the puppet state of Manchukuo, restoring the last Emperor, Pu Yi, to the throne. But it was only a pause, and the mass of the population was united in disgust and hatred at Japan's aggression and barbaric cruelty. The Communist Party issued major appeals to the nation to unite with it against Japan in 1934 and again on 1 August 1935. Ching-ling signed both of these, and on the latter she was joined by Sun Yat-sen's son, Sun Fo, and other luminaries.

Without any doubt, these appeals coincided entirely with Ching-ling's heartfelt stance. She was not only in touch with the Communist underground in Shanghai, but was on record as publicly backing the Communist administrations in the 'liberated areas'. But this support did not mean that Ching-ling did not have her own independent mind. She was not blind to some harsh facts. Harold Isaacs recalls her last words to him as he was taking his leave of her in 1934 after his 'parting of ways' with the Communists:

As we parted at her door, her final word was a warning to be careful. I thought she meant to be careful of Kuomintang thuggery. But no, she said, she meant our Communist friends. I looked at her incredulously. 'Yes,' she repeated, 'be careful. You don't really know these people. They are capable of anything.'

It should be added that Ching-ling was referring to a local Communist group, which was dominated by extremists. Edgar Snow wrote of her:

She was not without reservations in her acceptance of the party line. Once when I made some criticism of Trotsky, she suddenly smiled and went to her bookshelves. She pulled out Trotsky's newly published *The Revolution Betrayed*. 'There's a lot of truth in this,' she said, handing it to me. 'Read it.'

Ching-ling's position was that she took her own initiatives, but she supported the Communist Party in its attempt to unite the nation against the Japanese – and she shared the Communists' hatred and distrust of Chiang Kai-shek.

Chiang had adopted a fairly lofty stance towards Ching-ling, at least in public, while the 'mosquito press' slandered her and the Shanghai gangsters delivered none too subtle threats. Ching-ling, after all, was a member of the family, and Chiang was determined to hang on to his Soong connection. He may even not have wanted there to be too much gossip about her. However, some gesture was needed which would carry political force. When the Kuomintang next convened, in November 1935, Chiang saw to it that Ching-ling, who was still a full member of the Central Executive Committee, was demoted to alternate membership.

But the Kuomintang could not stand up against the tidal wave of popular feeling, either with gestures like demoting Ching-ling or by hurling its armies into repeated campaigns against the Communists. Its supine non-resistance in the face of Japan stirred up tremendous popular feeling which could not be contained by the police. On 9 December 1935 a mass student uprising broke out in Peking (known today as the 'December the 9th Movement'). These demonstrations were the largest Peking had ever seen, and they overtly supported the Communists' call for a 'united front'. Political protest spread and a boycott movement was launched against Japanese goods and personnel. Ching-ling put her weight firmly behind the December the 9th Movement.

Pressure built up all over China for a united front. One of the most important organizations involved was the All-China Federation of National Salvation ('Save the Nation!') Associations. On 31 May 1936 it issued a statement from the city of Sian near Yenan, calling for an end to non-resistance:

China has experienced four years and eight months of suffering. During this period Japanese imperialism . . . has lured our authorities into the trap of 'joint suppression of communism,' at the same time that it seizes from us a territory of 1,680,000 square kilometers, covering six provinces, enslaving sixty million of our people, and killing more than 300,000.

Seven leading members of the Association, who became known as 'the Seven Gentlemen' (although one of them was a woman, Shi Liang, who became Minister of Justice in the post-1949 government), were arrested and taken into custody in late November 1936 and imprisoned in the city of Soochow. Ching-ling initiated a 'go to prison to save the nation' movement. She and many others issued a declaration saying: 'If to love the country constitutes a crime, we want to be punished together with Shen Junru [one of the Seven] and the others; if it is not a crime, we want to share freedom with them.' In early July 1937 Ching-ling led a delegation to the Soochow prison, asking to be locked up alongside the Seven.

To some extent this was perhaps theatre. But it was effective theatre. Ching-ling used her immunity to 'stage' an event. She appeared to lay her own freedom on the line – and in a sense she did. By doing so, she was able, by playing subtly on the combination of personal constraints on Chiang and the rising tide in favour of resisting the Japanese, to make what was essentially a horrible situation much less horrible. At the end of the month the Seven were released.

The groundswell in favour of resisting the Japanese had reached right inside the Kuomintang itself. By early 1936 the key commander in north-west China, Chang Hsueh-liang, known as the 'Young Marshal', had decided to order his troops to stop fighting the Communists. In June he met secretly with the Communists' top negotiator, Chou En-lai. In early December Chiang Kai-shek flew to Sian where the situation was explosive, with mass demonstrations in support of the Young Marshal. When the Young Marshal and the local warlord, Yang Hu-cheng, failed to persuade Chiang to alter his policy and he tried to remove them, they kidnapped him and held him to ransom against a commitment to form a united front against the Japanese – in what became known as the 'Sian Incident'.

Chiang actually managed to escape the initial attempt to seize him, and fled up nearby Tiger Mountain, leaving his false teeth behind and badly damaging his back getting over a wall. After several hours hiding in a cave he was found and put under house arrest. The pro-Japanese faction in the government in Nanking threatened to bomb Sian 'to annihilate the rebels', with the implication that Chiang would be killed along with his captors. The Japanese were waiting for this opportunity to see China fall into total chaos. Long and tortuous negotiations ensued, involving the Soong family and the Communists in roles which have never been fully clarified. Chingling's brother T. V. Soong and her sister Mei-ling both flew to Sian, with the head of the Kuomintang secret police, Tai Li. Chou En-lai came down from Yenan. The Young Marshal wanted Chiang to sign an eight-point agreement guaranteeing to fight against Japan, to form a united front with the Communists and to restore democratic freedoms. Chiang refused.

Back in Yenan, Mao reportedly told a meeting of cadres that since the Shanghai massacre of 1927 'Chiang has owed us a blood debt as high as a mountain. Now is the time to liquidate the blood debt. Chiang must be brought to Pao-an for a public trial by the people of the whole country.' But while these fiery words were being spoken, Chou was sent to Sian to negotiate a compromise and demonstrate the Communists' statesmanlike face to the world. Chou firmly opposed the demand by Yang and Chang that Chiang Kai-shek be executed. Chiang and Mme Chiang were reported to be grateful to Chou for what he had done. It was the Soong family, in the persons of T. V. Soong and Mei-ling, who probably struck the final deal with Chou, and in fact it was the Communists who played the key role in solving the crisis. It is even possible they were instrumental in arranging the Incident in order to create a situation where they could force a compromise.

Chiang never would sign the eight-point agreement. He merely affirmed his commitment to it verbally. At the end of

December he was released. He treated his captors with his customary lack of mercy. The Young Marshal was placed under house arrest, where he remains (in Taiwan) to this day. As for General Yang, one of Chiang's last acts before he fled the mainland in 1949 was to sign his death warrant as well as those of all the surviving members of his family and his secretary's family.

After a decent interval so that Chiang could save some face after the indignity of his kidnapping, the Kuomintang government reached a tacit agreement with the Communists to cease the civil war and unite against the Japanese. In February 1937 the Kuomintang Central Executive Committee convened. On the 18th it was addressed by Ching-ling. She made a strong appeal for a united front, and publicly berated government leaders who were against stopping the civil war. Once again, she skilfully deployed the language and slogans which made her case virtually unanswerable, by making the appeal in the name of Sun Yat-sen and his Last Testament. The next day the Kuomintang officially called for the re-establishment of co-operation with both the Communist Party and the Soviet Union. The Communists were offering major concessions in return for national unity: the abandonment of the goal of overthrowing the Nanking regime; the dissolution of the Soviet government in the northwest; and the scrapping of their land reform policy. Even so, the Kuomintang dragged its feet for almost half a year, until on 7 July 1937 the Japanese launched an all-out assault on central and southern China. The Kuomintang then had to reach an accommodation with the Communists. A United Front was formed.

Ching-ling's independent, and spontaneous, attitude is illustrated by what she said to her brother-in-law H. H. Kung, when he came to her in the middle of the Sian negotiations and asked her to sign a statement denouncing the Young Marshal. Ching-ling retorted: 'What Chang Hsueh-liang did was right. I would have done the same thing if I had been in his place. *Only I would have gone further!*'

Ching-ling had devoted these six years in Shanghai to a sustained critique of Chiang and the Kuomintang. She clearly loathed Chiang. She had tried every means available to oppose him, most of all by using her relative immunity and her contacts. In 1936 she founded a new magazine, the *Voice of China*, to carry her message farther afield. When she was allowed to address the Kuomintang meeting in February 1937 she carried her swingeing criticisms right into the lion's jaws. She was not about to pull her punches with anyone, least of all members of her family, in spite of her emotional attachment to them.

In 1934, in order to try to improve the image of the Kuomintang, the Chiangs launched the New Life Movement, which was more to do with order and theatre than anything else. Ninety-six rules were promulgated relating to things like observing traffic regulations and washing one's hands before meals. Mme Chiang, in particular, tried to put a high-sounding gloss on the Movement – partly for American consumption.

But at a time of national emergency and social revolution, Ching-ling regarded this Movement as trivial and absurd. In early 1937 she published an article, appropriately enough in *Asia* magazine in New York, entitled 'Confucianism and

Modern China'; the New Life Movement, she said, was based on traditional Confucian philosophy which was by nature reactionary and she forcefully expressed her view that this was the exact opposite of what China needed at the time. The 'New Life Movement', she wrote, 'gives nothing to the people. Therefore, I propose to replace this pedantic movement by another . . . a revolutionary outlook on life rather than Confucianism . . .' Once again, she used the magic name of Sun Yat-sen and his teachings to discredit her opponents.

Many years later, in 1963, she summed up her feelings about these times:

The names of those who became traitors to [Sun's] Testament will remain forever hated in the annals of our nation and of mankind. Chiang Kai-shek and the other reactionaries in the ranks of the Kuomintang tore this document to shreds, then proceeded to line up with the imperialists against the Chinese people and the vital interests of our country. They filled a million graves with the best of our workers, peasants and revolutionary youth, as they began the fratricidal war and white terror which caused havoc to reign in our land and so weakened us that, when Japanese imperialism invaded China in 1931 and 1937, effective resistance was unbelievably difficult at the start.

CHAPTER FIVE

War against Japan (1937–45) and Civil War (1946–9)

On 7 July 1937 Japan created an 'incident' at Lukouchiao (Marco Polo Bridge), some ten miles south-west of Peking.

The next day Mao issued a manifesto calling for a war of resistance. Ten days later Chiang Kai-shek made a statement which Mao called 'the Kuomintang's first correct declaration on foreign affairs for many years', which also called for armed resistance and signalled an end to its long 'non-resistance' policy. The Sino-Japanese war was on.

In the next month, August, two articles appeared in American journals, one by Ching-ling, the other an interview with her sister Mme Chiang. Mme Chiang was apparently still obsessed with her old favourites. According to her interviewer, Fulton Oursler, she said the regeneration of China was to be achieved 'especially by the ideals embodied in the New Life Movement'. Oursler observed: 'I could see from the sudden excited look on Madame's face that in this movement . . . were all her mind and heart and soul.'

In contrast, Ching-ling's article was a fiery and indignant statement, 'China Unconquerable', in a completely different mood from the Kuomintang pessimism: 'It is my confident belief that China not only can resist every and any Japanese aggression but that she can and must prepare to recover her lost territories.' She had no truck with the sort of 'blackmail' Chiang formulated to get American aid. He put his case passively:

We hope to be able to secure supplies to enable us to keep on indefinitely. If the Democratic States do not see to it that provision is made to this end, then a time will come when they will regret allowing Japan to defeat China ...

While Ching-ling dramatically declared: 'No! China could not be defeated even if she had to fight Japan single-handed.' Throughout the article, Ching-ling was urging: 'Co-operation between the Kuomintang and the Communist Party is absolutely essential. All forces must be united.' Interestingly, she used here the expression 'paper tiger' in English to describe 'the might of Japan' – an expression which Mao employed much later, in 1946, to refer to America's atom bomb and which then became famous as his coinage.

On 22 and 23 September the Kuomintang Central News Agency released a declaration of the Communist Party and a statement of the Kuomintang, respectively, both announcing the establishment of co-operation between the two parties. The United Front was thus proclaimed. The Chinese Soviet government dissolved itself and continued as an autonomous regional regime. The Red Army became the 'Eighth Route' and 'New Fourth' armies under Chiang's nominal command.

In November 1937, when the Shanghai area fell into the hands of the Japanese, Ching-ling left the city for Hong Kong. In June 1938 she founded the China Defence League, which she defined as 'concerned entirely with relief'. The money and relief materials she collected became the main outside supply for the Communist-controlled areas.

The Communist armies were waging a remarkably effective guerrilla war against the Japanese, continually recovering occupied territories, and expanding their power and influence.

In spite of the formation of the United Front, the relationship between the Communists and the Kuomintang was harmonious only in appearance. At heart it was antagonistic. In fact, Chiang was trying to isolate and contain the Communists. He deployed half a million soldiers to seal off the main Communist region, in the north-west. This was one of the most barren areas in China and the Communists were badly in need of supplies of every kind.

Ching-ling did her best to get relief goods through. George Hatem, the American doctor who went to Yenan with Edgar Snow in 1936, wrote:

Altogether, with her constant support, we organized 11 International Peace Hospitals with 42 mobile units at the fronts, and eight medical schools. Also under her influence many foreign doctors came to China, including Norman Bethune, D. Kotnis, B. K. Basu, Drs Atal and Cholkar, and Hans Muller.

... Among the things she sent us were materials and directions for making penicillin – at that time new in the world ... [which was] extremely valuable in the treatment of infections, for pus cavities in lungs and for osteomyelitis.

The Communists were grateful for Ching-ling's timely help – what the Chinese call 'sending charcoal in snowy weather'. Not all the goods reached their destination, though. More often than not they were confiscated by the blockading Kuomintang armies.

But Ching-ling let these events pass without public comment. She refrained from any direct criticisms of the Kuomintang. She was at the time, as the writer John Gunther put it, 'outside the *grande ligne* of Chinese politics'; she led a quiet and busy life, burying herself in the daily routine of collecting and sending relief materials.

When the Chinese Industrial Co-operatives (the Gung Ho movement) were set up by Ching-ling, Nym Wales (Helen Snow), Edgar Snow, Rewi Alley and others, as part of the war effort, Ching-ling became President of the Hong Kong Promotion Committee. In Hong Kong she lived in borrowed flats and houses. She had few personal possessions. She sold all the jewellery her mother had left her to raise money for relief work. Luxury to her was criminal in a poor country at war like China. In this she set herself off decisively from the insensitive extravagance of her sister, Mme Chiang. When Mei-ling went to America to plead for the impoverished Chinese, her luggage was full of cosmetics, lingerie and fur coats. The GIs on the US planes were furious at having to carry her special purchases and on at least one occasion dropped and broke the crates carrying her belongings and kicked her fur coats round in the dust.

Ching-ling's ascetic life-style won her moral prestige. Gunther was not the only one to write of her with admiration:

She could have had almost any position for the asking. At great cost of physical hardship, she gave up everything for what she said her husband stood for. She gave up family, wealth, and privilege. Few women ever gave up more. Her friends have repeatedly offered to buy her a motorcar, to make it easier for her to live. She has refused to accept anything, and gives every penny she has to relief work ...

By the end of 1938 Chiang had set up his wartime capital in the 'mountain city' Chungking in Szechwan Province, one of the most remote and inaccessible parts of China, where 'the mountains are so high that even the emperor cannot reach'. But Ching-ling did not want to go and live there in open co-operation with Chiang.

Her steel will often caused false expectations. Gunther met her at this time:

I expected to find a sort of Queen Victoria, a resigned and perhaps forbidding figure, widow's weeds and all. But Madame Sun, even to-day, looks like a girl of twenty-eight. Her grace and vivacity, frail as she is, as well as the carved perfection of her features, gave an impression not of a historic revolutionary character, but of a young woman at the threshold of a career.

Ching-ling's appearance was not misleading. She was at heart vivacious and tender. Now that civil strife had given way formally to a United Front, it was much easier for her to enjoy the company of her family.

In February 1940 Mei-ling, Mme Chiang Kai-shek, went to Hong Kong 'for health reasons'. She stayed with Ai-ling. According to the sisters' biographer, Emily Hahn:

Madame Sun too moved in ... for a few happy days the three sisters completely forgot their public roles. It was the first time in many years that they were able to sink political differences with free consciences; the United Front was a fact in that house. They gossiped, they cooked, they made jokes – the old family jokes that outsiders can never understand – they tried on one another's clothes ...

Then one day Hahn (who was known as 'Mickey') was sent for by Ai-ling: '"My sisters have persuaded me to come out to dinner," she said excitedly. "We are going to dine at the Hong Kong Hotel tonight, and I thought that it would be worth seeing us all together ..."' Hahn went with an RAF officer: 'Mme Sun, sober in black, looked at us appraisingly and said to Mme Kung, "There's Mickey Hahn. I suppose that's Mickey Mouse she's with?"'

The news that the three sisters were dining together was a bombshell. Hahn describes the scene:

Word went around quickly and in a few moments the dance floor looked something like the crowd at Wimbledon as couples danced past the long table, their heads turning as if they had owls' necks, staring as hard as British courtesy allowed ...

'I'll believe two of them are there,' protested a newspaperman, 'but I won't believe that's Madame Sun. She would never, never be with the other two – and in this outpost of Empire!'

'It's Finland,' said another man emphatically. 'You mark my words, It's Finland. She must be completely disgusted with Russia now, and this is a reaction – it's all Finland.'

'No, it isn't,' said the first suddenly. 'I know what it is. It's Wang Ching-wei.'

They turned and stared again at the wall table, at three Chinese ladies who sat quietly eating their dinners ...

The man whose name the newspaperman mentioned, Wang Ching-wei, had been a leader of the Kuomintang government and had recently left Chungking and was collaborating with the Japanese. The time of the dinner was close to Wang's inauguration as the puppet head of Japanese-occupied China. Ching-ling's appearance in public with her sisters gave people reassurance that the United Front was still solid.

For this reason, Ching-ling agreed to go to Chungking with her sisters. She arrived there on 1 April 1940: 'the first time in years', as Hahn observed, 'that she had visited any stamping ground of the National government'. She stayed in Ai-ling's mansion. During the entire length of her stay her activities were headlines in the papers all over China. Together with her sisters she inspected factories and hospitals. Films were made of them visiting dugouts and orphanages. They went on a much-publicized two-day trip to Chengtu during which the city was bombed several times by the Japanese; even this was interpreted as a deliberate reaction to the sisters' reunion. When Ching-ling was photographed with Chiang in the act of toasting him, the United Front seemed secure.

But behind the blaze of publicity Ching-ling remained reserved. She had not forgotten the unbridgeable political chasm that lay between herself and her hosts. As she stated after the war: 'I avoided political controversy lest it injure this work [resistance]. I kept silent because all attention had to be centred in winning the war.' Presumably for this reason she did not see very much of the left-wing young enthusiasts in Chungking.

On 18 April 1940 the three sisters made broadcasts to America. Ching-ling spent half the time giving credit to her sister Ai-ling. She appeared positively co-operative with the

Kuomintang. Yet, from the unusual brevity and self-effacing style of her speech in comparison with those of her sisters, one could feel she was cautious.

At the beginning of May 1940 Ching-ling left Chungking and went back to Hong Kong where she resumed her work with the China Defence League. The Secretary of the League was the daughter of Liao Chung-kai and Ho Hsiang-ning, the left-wing Kuomintang leader, and was a member of the Communist Party. Through her and her brother, then the top Communist official in Hong Kong, Ching-ling kept in constant contact with the Communists.

In the course of the war, in spite of the United Front, the old scores between the Communists and the Kuomintang got even worse. Chiang told the American journalist Theodore White: 'The Japanese are a disease of the skin, the Communists are a disease of the heart.' Chiang took numerous measures to prevent the Communists from growing stronger. In addition to the blockade in the north-west, his troops had been causing 'frictions' with the Communist-led New Fourth Army in the south. Mao instructed his armies that in those circumstances they had to 'stress struggle and not unity ... to reach out into all enemy [Japanese]-occupied areas and not to be bound by the Kuomintang's restrictions but to go beyond the limits allowed by the Kuomintang ...'

In January 1941 Chiang ordered a surprise attack on the New Fourth Army in which thousands of soldiers were massacred. Theodore White called the incident 'the King Charles's head of the Chinese civil war'. The United Front was thereafter a mere name.

Ching-ling sent a strong telegram of protest to Chiang. After that she renewed her criticisms of the Chiang government, though often not by name. In October 1941, in an article for *Asia* magazine in New York, she talked about 'incendiaries of civil war [who] might again rend our country and open wide the gates to the enemy'. In November 1941 she wrote an article on the tenth anniversary of the death of Teng Yen-ta. By choosing this moment to mourn her old friend publicly with intense sorrow, she left little doubt about how acutely she felt.

In early December 1941 it became obvious in Hong Kong that war was drawing near there, too. Many people were trying to persuade Ching-ling to leave. Sun Yat-sen's body-guard, Morris Cohen, was one of them. On 2 December he arrived from Chungking.

As soon as we touched down, I went to her house. There I bumped up against the hardest of all brick walls – the obstinacy of a really good woman. Up to the day of the Great Doctor's death she'd always done what he said was right. Since then she'd always done what she thought was right. She saw no reason to change now. It was no good trying to argue with her ...

'If there is fighting here, there will be wounded, there will be refugees and children will suffer. Perhaps I may be able to help them. I shall stay right here!'

That was all. It was quite enough. The days went by. I called on her every morning and sat down in her drawing-room and talked my head off. All she did was to smile and repeat, 'My duty is to stay here.'

The following weekend the Japanese attacked Hong Kong.

I played my last card. I went once more to Mme Sun and told her that she must realize she was a sort of national heroine to the Chinese people. If she stayed here while the fortress fell (as it had to fall, sooner or later), a lot of Chinese would take arms to defend her person to the death. She'd be the cause of a lot of unnecessary slaughter. That was an argument she could appreciate. She promised to leave as soon as a plane was available.

The following night a few transport planes got in from the north. I took the two sisters across to the mainland and saw them off. It was a pretty grim farewell. We all knew that it was likely to be our last. For once I found myself absolutely tongue-tied. I couldn't think what the hell to say. We shook hands, and I just blurted out, 'We'll fight to the bitter end, anyway.'

She stopped on the steps of the ramp, looked down at me and said, 'We'll fight, too, Morris. but not to the *bitter* end. The end, when it comes. will be sweet!'

It was the last plane to leave Hong Kong. Next day the airport fell to the Japanese.

Ching-ling lived in Chungking until the end of the war. Throughout this period she remained in deep seclusion. She was under close surveillance, unlike during her previous stay, as she had resumed her strong public criticism of the Chiang government.

Chiang did not have a particularly good record during the war. General Joseph ('Vinegar Joe') Stilwell said: 'It would of course have been undiplomatic to go into the nature of the military effort Chiang Kai-shek had made since 1938. It was practically zero.'

One of the defence measures the Kuomintang took against the Japanese was to blow up the dikes on the Yellow River. They gave no advance warning to the local population.

Several thousand villages were flooded and millions were made homeless. This slowed the Japanese down for only a few months. Another part of the war effort was to collect grain taxes which were more than the land had raised in grain, and many years in advance, even in areas which were already suffering from famine. George Adams, an American relief worker, spoke to the British journalist Stuart Gelder:

'Millions of people there [in Kwangtung] are dying of starvation,' he said. 'I've seen them. I've just come back – millions of them, in their houses, in the fields, on the roads, everywhere. They're eating earth and the bark of trees. That's bad enough – but it's worse than that. They're going crazy. They're killing children and eating them.'

I suppose he caught my expression of stupefied unbelief as I received these bursts of words in my face before I even had time to show him to a chair. He apologized. 'Don't get me wrong. I don't mean they're killing and eating their *own* children. They're exchanging children for other people's so they don't have to kill their own.'

Theodore White saw similar things in Honan:

... It took five days to get through to Chiang K'ai-shek, and then only with the help of his sister-in-law, the sainted widow of Dr Sun Yat-sen ... [She] stiffened me for the meeting with a last note, in which she set up the appointment. '... I was told,' she wrote me, 'that he [Chiang] was very weary after his long tedious inspection tour and needed a few days' rest. But I insisted that the matter involved the lives of many millions ... May I suggest that you report conditions as frankly and fearlessly as you did to me. If heads must come off, don't be squeamish about it ... otherwise there would be no change in the situation.'

Chiang used this situation to appeal for more American

aid. America poured in billions of US dollars in various forms. In Britain, a popular wartime radio comedy actually featured a character named 'General Cash My Cheque'. In a talk with Stuart Gelder, Ching-ling showed her anger:

> There isn't going to be [any fighting] ... my brother-in-law is keeping the guns the Americans have given him in grease until they have beaten the Japanese for him. Then he will unwrap them for the war in which he's really interested, against the Communists.

Relief funds and supplies also fell into another hole – chiefly the pockets of the extended Soong family. President Truman did not mince his words (after he left office):

> Any money we spent to support them would end up ... a good deal of it would end up in the pockets of Chiang and the Madame and the Soong and Kung families ... They stole it – and it's invested in real estate down in Sao Paulo and some right here in New York.

But Ching-ling was indefatigable in trying to keep supplies flowing to the Communist areas. Her China Defence League, which set up office in Chungking soon after she moved there, was almost wholly involved in collecting materials for the Communist armies. In an 'open letter to friends of China abroad' on 18 September 1943 Ching-ling explained the reason with acute indignation:

An internal political blockade denies them doctors, surgical instruments and drugs, even those that are sent by friends abroad. We do not ask for these forces to receive preferential treatment. We ask for equality of treatment, for a stop to the practice, and to the acquiescence of others in the practice, that has drawn an imaginary line through China on one side of which a soldier wounded in the fight against Japan is assumed to be entitled to have his wounds healed, and on the other, not.

Ching-ling's influence on international opinion led to a form of detention. A US officer, John Service, reported on a visit to Ching-ling in Chungking in February 1944:

> She was more outspoken and apparently nearer to being bitter than on any of the previous four or five times that I had met her ...
>
> She has recently been invited by 'several organizations' to visit the United States ... She had planned to accept this invitation and hoped to leave early in March. She has, however, been bluntly told that she will not be permitted to go abroad.
>
> She believes the reason for this refusal is the violent reaction of her family and high Kuomintang officials to the publication in *Reynold's Weekly*, a British Labor magazine, of a report that she had sent a message to bodies in the United States, describing the blockade against the Communists and calling for its removal ... Following the receipt in Chungking of copies of the article, she was separately visited by [three top Kuomintang officials]. Their line, which she characterized as childish lecturing, was to upbraid her for 'spreading baseless rumors,' 'appealing to foreigners,' 'washing China's dirty linen in the foreign press,' and so on ...
>
> She mentioned that her family was 'very annoyed ...'
>
> ... I could not help getting the impression that Madame Sun's position is now a strained and difficult one and that she is more than ever a prisoner. She implied this in a rather defiant remark when discussing the displeasure over her efforts to have the anti-Communist blockade lifted: 'All they can do is to keep me from traveling.'

Ching-ling was also the sole public critic in Chungking of

the Kuomintang's continuing repression. As the American ambassador observed in March 1944: 'no Chinese of any importance has dared to give voice publicly even by implication to the existence of such conditions except Madame Sun.' She repeated her charges to American Vice-President Henry Wallace when he visited China in mid-1944 on a fact-finding mission. Ching-ling's reputation as a 'red' meant that her voice was ignored by the US government. It also sealed her off from most Chinese in Chungking. Service reported: 'She did not go out much in Chungking. People were able to go in and see her, but they had to be willing to be in the doghouse. She was regarded as being outside the pale.' The American writer Sterling Seagrave found out:

According to US army intelligence reports during the war, when she staged soccer matches, Chiang's security people warned fans not to attend, and definitely not to root for Ching-ling's team, under fear of arrest.

The United Front, as had been symbolized by her family reunion, was now a mere façade. She gave Helen Snow a 'family snap' in which a very reserved Ching-ling is to be seen standing beside a grinning Chiang Kai-shek and her sisters. Inscribed on the back was 'UF' (United Front).

On 15 August 1945 the Sino-Japanese war ended with the unconditional surrender of Japan. Chiang Kai-shek had been waiting for this day to get at his real enemy. Mao reminded his Party on 13 August that Chiang was 'a most brutal and treacherous fellow' who wanted to repeat the history of 1927. Chiang Kai-shek had swords in both hands, said Mao. 'We take up swords, too, following his example.' In the forthcoming contest, there was no doubt with whom Ching-ling stood. In December 1945 she left Chungking for Shanghai, where she reorganized her China Defence League into the China Welfare Fund, which mainly helped children and Communist-oriented intellectuals.

In the meantime peace negotiations of a kind were going on. The Communists had by then grown strong enough to challenge the Kuomintang. Their armies had expanded from just over 40,000 men in 1937 to over one million and they had set up many bases in areas taken from the Japanese. What is more, they had won the heart of the nation. Nevertheless, Chiang's army still outnumbered the Communist forces; and Chiang had America's dollars behind him. There were numerous small-scale clashes to interrupt the 'peace-talks'. On 26 June 1946 all-out civil war erupted.

Ching-ling appealed for a coalition government. She condemned the Kuomintang's policies and called for 'the American people to stop their government from militarily aiding the Kuomintang'. Mao said the same thing in an interview with Anna Louise Strong in August 1946.

In the final showdown, the Kuomintang made a last-ditch attempt to gain some sort of support, or at least neutrality, from Ching-ling, knowing the weight attached to her name. It kept elevating her official position. She was reinstated to full membership on the Central Executive Committee in 1945, promoted to the Standing Committee the next year, and appointed an adviser to the government the year after. Ching-ling angrily refused to lend her name to these manoeuvres: 'I have no intention whatsoever in engaging in political campaigns for joining the [Nationalist] government.'

At the end of 1947 some dissidents in the Kuomintang drew up a plan to set up a 'Kuomintang Revolutionary Committee' in Hong Kong. They wrote a long letter to Ching-ling, asking her to head the Committee. She agreed to be the honorary president.

Chiang was by now fighting a losing war against the Communists. The Kuomintang's performance was animatedly described by ex-President Truman:

> They weren't any damn good, never had been. We sent them about three billion five hundred million dollars' worth of *matériel*, sent that to the so-called free Chinese, and then about five million of Chiang's men between Peking and Nanking surrendered to three hundred thousand Communists, and the Communists used that *matériel* to run Chiang and his men out of China. I told you. He never was any damn good.
>
> They wanted me to send in about five million Americans to rescue him, but I wouldn't do it. There wasn't *anything* that could be done to save him, and he was as corrupt as they come. I wasn't going to waste one single American life to save him, and I didn't care what they said. They hooted and hollered and carried on and said I was soft on Communism and I don't know what all. But I never gave in on that, and I never changed my mind about Chiang and his gang. Every damn one of them ought to be in jail, and I'd like to live to see the day they are.

The Communist victory came with a speed that surprised even themselves. This was largely to do with the enthusiastic support of the people, one demonstration of which was the collapse of morale in the Kuomintang armies. Increasing numbers of Kuomintang soldiers began to surrender or let themselves be captured. By the end of the civil war, casualties amounted to less than 20 per cent of total Kuomintang losses. In the climactic moment, according to O. Edmund Clubb, then US Consul General in Peking, when a large force of crack Kuomintang troops was surrounded, 'the proposal was put forward [at Nanking headquarters] to destroy the valuable heavy equipment of the fated force by air bombardment – *in situ*, regardless of the consequences for the Nationalist troops.' The doomed force learned of the proposal and surrendered forthwith. Immediately after this battle, on 21 January 1949, on the eve of the surrender of Peking, Chiang 'retired' and was succeeded by Vice-President Li Tsung-jen. Li (who went over to the mainland in the 1960s) solicited Ching-ling's 'leadership in the Party and national affairs'. She turned the request down flat. With her summary refusal came the landslide collapse of the Kuomintang. In May 1949 Chiang fled to Taiwan.

CHAPTER SIX

The People's Republic: 1949–66

When the Communists arrived in Shanghai in May 1949, Ching-ling remained. Her whole family had left or fled China by then. Her sisters and brothers were in the USA. Sun Fo, her stepson, went to France. She alone chose the Communists.

The whole nation welcomed the Communists. Mao promised a clean and capable government, a bright and exciting future. Ching-ling shared the nation's enthusiasm.

On 1 July 1949, the twenty-eighth anniversary of the founding of the Chinese Communist Party, Ching-ling made a speech at a grand celebration in Shanghai. It was a passionate song of praise: 'This is the new light in our land. Freedom is dawning. It is spreading its warmth into every reactionary-darkened corner ... A salute to the people's freedom!' The Communist Party was then preparing for the inauguration of the People's Republic and had chosen Peking as the new capital. Mao Tse-tung and Chou En-lai beseeched Ching-ling in personal letters to come to Peking and join the new government. Mme Chou was sent as the bearer of the letters to Shanghai. At first Ching-ling declined. She said that Peking was a sad place for her as Sun Yat-sen had died there. But she was readily convinced by Mme Chou. (The Chinese would never accept an invitation first time out of almost ritualistic politeness.) She arrived in the new capital by train on 1 September 1949. She was met on the platform by a host of the highest Communist leaders: Mao, Chou, Liu Shao-chi, Chu Teh and others.

Ching-ling was subsequently given a number of posts, of which the most important was as one of the six vice-presidents of the Central People's Government Council, the highest organ of state authority, chaired by Mao. On 1 October she stood on the famous Tien An Men Gate in Peking, together with Mao and other state leaders, for the inauguration of the People's Republic. Her description of the day was full of exuberance:

It was a solemn, awe-inspiring ceremony. My heart was filled with overflowing joy. Waves of memories surged over my mind. I was thinking of the many comrades who had sacrificed their lives for our victory today. I seemed to be seeing all those years of struggles and hardship. One thought held my heart tight: all that was in the past and would never happen again. Today, Sun Yat-sen's efforts at last bore fruit – and such beautiful fruit too!

The new-born People's Republic was permeated with a festive atmosphere. Ching-ling was swept up into the spontaneous festivities. She observed how Peking citizens gathered on Tien An Men Square to celebrate: '... torches changed night into broad daylight. China has now learned to sing and dance!'

She turned out many articles and speeches in the years immediately following the Liberation – the longest being an enthusiastic report after an inspection tour of the north-east.

They were mostly passionate, unreserved eulogies of the new China and bore no resemblance to the angry and fierce writings tirelessly attacking Chiang Kai-shek. She found her home in the People's Republic. From then on she shared the sweetness and the bitterness of the people there.

But just when China desperately wanted a period of peace to rebuild its war-ravaged economy, the Korean War broke out in 1950. The Chinese thought that the Americans were attempting to use Korea as a springboard for the invasion of China to restore Chiang Kai-shek to power. The nation was filled with indignation. Some three million 'volunteers' were sent to fight in Korea, and back in China many parents gave their new-born babies names like 'Resist the Americans', 'Help Korea' and 'Peace'.

Ching-ling fiercely attacked the US intervention in Korea and was prominently involved in the international left-wing peace campaign. She won the Stalin Peace Prize in 1951 (which was duly recorded in her FBI dossier).

In 1952, when a volume of her texts was published in English in Peking (*The Struggle for New China*), Ching-ling dedicated it 'To the Korean People's Army and the Chinese People's Volunteers'. In December that year she headed the Chinese delegation to the Congress of Peoples for Peace held in Vienna. There she sat on a platform with Brecht, Sartre, Aragon, Ehrenburg and other radical luminaries.

She took an active part in the campaign denouncing America for using germ warfare in Korea and north-east China. When the Indian journalist Frank Moraes, who had known her in wartime Chungking, visited her in her office in Shanghai in 1952, she had up on one wall a caricature of US

Secretary of State, Dean Acheson, 'as a tentacled bug holding a parchment of peace in one hand and hugging a container of bacterial bugs in the other. Madame Sun pointed to the drawing and laughed.'

Along with her role in the international peace movement she was also active in promoting Sino-Soviet friendship, and was one of the very last foreigners to meet Stalin, in mid-January 1953, on her way back from Vienna. Stalin's first (and only recorded) words to her were: 'The Chinese people are a good people.'

The first five years of the People's Republic were a period of economic recovery after the devastating war. Land reform was carried out. The speed of the recovery was stunning – owing, largely, to the whole-hearted co-operation of the nation.

By late 1956 China had completed what was called 'Socialist transformation'. Industry and commerce were in effect taken over by the state; farming was in the process of being gradually collectivized. The process ran smoothly on the whole. The majority of the population believed that the fundamental cause of poverty in old China was private ownership of the means of production; they placed their hope in a new system of public ownership. Indeed, the following year, 1957, was one of the best in terms of economic growth.

Socialism fulfilled part of Ching-ling's dreams. She said: 'I firmly believe that in the future socialism and ultimately communism will become universal social systems.'

The Communist Party was enjoying its best image at that time and many personalities and intellectuals were joining it. In early 1957 Ching-ling told Liu Shao-chi that she wanted to join the Party. The Communist leadership was delighted. But they declined the request as her enthusiastically support-ive voice would carry more weight if she were not a Party member.

Encouraged by their impressive success, the Communists felt confident enough to invite criticisms, attempting some kind of democracy. But they failed to anticipate the possibility of criticisms that challenged some of the Party's fundamen-tals. Party officials panicked as though they were letting the genie out of the bottle. They hastily started an 'anti-Rightist campaign' to silence and condemn all critics, most of whom were intellectuals. The great irony was that there were actually very few real dissidents at the time. Most people who criticized the party were in fact firm supporters. They merely wanted to do it a service. Among the condemned, some had even spent sleepless nights trying to think of something to complain about in order to please the Party. Among these was one of the famous 'Seven Gentlemen', Wang Zao-shi.

Wang and most other 'Rightists' were not imprisoned or shot. Their punishment was 'lenient' – mainly ostracism. Few had then experienced the fact that ostracism, which hit the entire family, and which indeed very often came from one's own family members, was laceratingly hard to bear. Few realized that the 'humane' treatment, under which the 'Rightists' were not divorced by their spouses, was the cruel-lest of all: the spouses of the 'Rightists' were discriminated against and were constantly 'educated' with the idea that they were living with a 'class enemy' whom they ought to hate. Both parties had to carry two crosses with no hope of ever being relieved. This turned many a loving couple into bitter enemies.

The campaign was the beginning of a period of darkness. For many it came as the first storm of icy water on the fire of their revolutionary passion, the first challenge to their ideals. For most, fear began to prevail – fear of saying something wrong, or of saying something that might unexpectedly be regarded as wrong, even many years later.

How did Ching-ling take this campaign? Outwardly, she stood by the side of the Party when it first started to invite criticisms, and subsequently when it clamped down on alleged dissidents. One of her articles in 1957 at the height of the campaign was entitled 'To Repudiate the Leadership of the Communist Party is to Drag the Chinese People Down to the Gutter of Slavery'. In her address to the Third National Congress of Chinese Women in 1957 she called for women to 'overcome undue softheartedness and thoroughly smash bourgeois Rightists'. Her other public speeches and articles also demonstrated unwavering support for the Party.

Did she, then, not have any reservations?

She had fiercely attacked Chiang Kai-shek's one-Party dictatorship. She had advocated democracy as an essential part of Sun Yat-sen's legacy. She must have known that people like Wang Zao-shi, who had been imprisoned by the Kuomintang for his outspoken spirit, had nothing but good will towards the People's Republic. Now they were being punished for mere critical suggestions, which had actually been solicited – and allegedly in an atmosphere of freedom. How did she justify all this? It appeared that Ching-ling was behaving in one manner under the Kuomintang and quite another under the Communists. Such self-contradiction seems to be a constant and common phenomenon in Communist societies. One part of the explanation is, possibly, that Communism is most likely to emerge in societies where conditions are such that a life-and-death struggle is inevitable, where people have no choice but to take sides. The 'third way' is a dead end. China was a society of this kind. Ching-ling took sides – with the Communists, as she believed that they were the successors to Sun Yat-sen's revolution. In 1956 she said the Communists 'have not only transferred Sun's life-long dreams into reality, but achieved much more than Sun's ideals'. After going through a sea of suffering and blood, it is not easy for people to give up their ideals, or their side. When wrongs and evils spring up in the name of these ideals, they either close their eyes, or try to find excuses. Besides, there is always the argument that one must not give any help to 'the enemy'. In a way, those who have fought for their ideals eventually become captives of these ideals.

Nineteen fifty-eight was the year of the 'Great Leap Forward' and the 'People's Communes', when Mao put into practice his implacable determination to remould the Chinese people. Mao expressed his ideas in striking terms:

Apart from their other characteristics, China's 600 million people have two remarkable peculiarities; they are, first of all, poor, and secondly blank. That may seem like a bad thing, but it is really a good thing. Poor people want change, want to do things, want revolution. A clean sheet of paper has no blotches, and so the newest and most beautiful words can be written on it, the newest and most beautiful pictures can be painted on it.

Mao, no doubt, saw himself as the writer and the painter.

The dominant belief in the country was that China needed only some fifteen to twenty years of industrialization to surpass the West by such means as getting the entire population to produce iron and steel in 'backyard furnaces'; and that agriculture could grow in leaps and bounds by the organization of peasants into communes where they would work whenever they liked and get paid whatever they needed. These fantasies resulted in excessive targets and gross exaggerations. As an absurd example, communes claimed that their fields could grow ten times more rice than before. They planted crops ten times more densely for the inspectors. The fields often ended up producing next to nothing. This unbridled recklessness partly caused the ensuing great famine between 1959 and 1961 and cost millions of lives.

Ching-ling went along with this crazy business. She was said to have had a blast furnace put up in her garden. Khrushchev mentions it in his memoirs: 'I don't know whether she ever produced any pig iron from her furnace, but she showed it off and bragged about it to visitors.' But Ching-ling must have had her reservations. Indeed, she wrote a letter (not for publication) correcting a boastful account of China's welfare work for a magazine – a rare event at the time.

While an almost childish fever was spreading over the country, the Defence Minister, Peng Teh-huai, and his friends stood up and criticized Mao. They were branded as an 'Anti-Party Group' in July 1959, and their supporters as 'Right Opportunists'. Ching-ling gave no hint of supporting them publicly. Harsh reality was not audible in her voice during this period. She enunciated the same line as the Communist Party and voiced only high-sounding optimism. But she may have contributed offstage to the Party's decision to change course. From the winter of 1960 most 'Right Opportunists' had their labels removed. A number of pragmatic economic measures were taken. As a result, the economy flourished, and there was a nationwide positive and joyful atmosphere.

Ching-ling was working actively. Even the painful leukaemia which had been diagnosed a few years earlier seemed to take a turn for the better. On the eve of 1966 she wrote a long article summarizing the sixteen years of the People's Republic. The Communist Party, she concluded, had 'brought the Chinese people many historic victories'.

For all her commitment, Ching-ling was not substantially involved in policy-making. Her role was more honorary and symbolic. She had prestige, which was a tribute to her long years of fighting on the side of the Communists. Her mere presence on the mainland gave the Communists endorsement as the legitimate successors to Sun Yat-sen's revolution. In this sense, power automatically attached itself to her. But she had no authority to control events or decide the direction of development. Apparently, she did not mind being in this role. Unlike Mao's wife, Chiang Ching, who claimed to the American writer Roxane Witke, 'Writing's your area of expertise. Mine is revolutionary leadership!', Ching-ling was never a seeker after power for herself. As Harold Isaacs put it: 'This, more than anything else, enabled her to confront the complexities of all the politics of her years without being diminished by them.'

There is perhaps another reason for Ching-ling's equanimity about holding only a nominal position at the top of the State. She knew her own limitations – a valuable but not readily found quality. Among comments made about her these two by Helen Snow are emblematic:

> Mme Sun had to have a mind of her own and she did have, though she is not an intellectual type but rather emotional and intuitive.

> Mme Sun is a great woman not for what she has done but for what she has not done. She is respected for what she is not for any great accomplishment.

Not to be charged with undue responsibility may have come as a relief for her. Over the years she had been fighting not for power, but for her conscience. Now it seemed that her conscience was by and large at ease. She was content to be in a supporting position to the Communist Party.

She was active in the official women's movement. From the time of the founding of the All-China Women's Federation in 1949, she was continuously its honorary president. And in this field her ideas on women's liberation did help to shape policies.

In the People's Republic the position of women was dramatically different from what it had been in the past. Special laws were brought in to protect women's rights and these were effectively applied. In the advanced areas women probably enjoyed more equality than in most countries of the world. All women of working age worked outside the home and received equal pay. It was normal for men to do housework as well as women. The concept of 'housewife' became outdated and actually acquired an undesirable connotation.

On the other hand, the approach of emphasizing women as a 'social element', as 'individual persons', rather than as the 'female sex' contributed to a kind of outward desexualization of society. On practical issues Ching-ling's sense of sexual equality embraced vasectomy; she told a friend: 'After all, why should women bear all the burden?'

Her chief day-to-day activities lay in welfare work. In 1950 she reorganized the China Welfare Fund and changed its name to the China Welfare Institute, focusing on the welfare of children. Having lost her only child by miscarriage in 1922, she transferred her affection to children at large.

The China Welfare Institute also published a foreign-language periodical, *China Reconstructs*, founded by Ching-ling in 1952, which was one of the few major voices of China overseas. Her care for the journal was meticulous, as Israel Epstein, editor-in-chief and a close friend of hers, recalled:

On international journeys, she made small purchases for our work. For instance, in a note from Lahore, Pakistan, on her 1956 tour of South Asia, she wrote, 'Pardon penciled scrawl – a thousand things to attend to but must get this off to you. It was simply impossible to obtain nylon typewriter ribbons in all the three countries visited ... However, here is a Remington ribbon ...' (In the 1950s Chinese typewriter ribbons were still poorly inked and did not wear well.)

Ching-ling's irreplaceable role and unique contribution went far beyond her specific work and transcended her symbolic status. In 1957 when Mao was going to the Moscow meeting of World Communist Parties he made a point of taking Ching-ling on the delegation. She was the only non-

Communist representative at the Conference. Mao had her sitting beside him when he signed the declaration at the end.

Devoted to her people, charismatic and sophisticated, she projected the best image of China. She went on a number of goodwill tours overseas and made a tremendously favourable impression. James Bertram remarked:

Pandit Nehru's voice, when he greeted her in Delhi [in 1955], had a tone which does not occur in his speeches of welcome to European visitors. 'Whatever storms and tempests shook China in these last years,' he said then, 'her faith never faltered. Her voice was always raised for peace ...'

Nehru had photographs of two women in his chambers. One was of his late wife. The other was of Mme Sun.

At home a great deal of her time was spent receiving foreign dignitaries. More than one of them left with the comment that the Chinese Communists must have something to say for themselves if they attracted personalities like her.

She also became a kind of authority among the leadership on the West. She provided a taste, an understanding, for Western ways which was rare, particularly in those days when China was rather isolated. At her dinner table one might get macaroni with cheese, American style, which Ching-ling announced as 'the house speciality'. After dinner there was coffee, instead of green tea, sometimes served with Cointreau, which was her favourite liqueur. Mme Liu Shao-chi recalled with nostalgia how Ching-ling offered to teach her to make coffee. Before state visits abroad with her husband, who was the President of China, she always wrote to Mme Sun to ask how she should dress, talk and socialize.

Ching-ling would write her detailed instructions before the Lius went on a foreign tour: 'Turn off the air-conditioning before you go to sleep so as not to catch cold', 'Don't eat too much raw or cold food', etc.

The Communist government appreciated Ching-ling's contribution and responded with care and thoughtfulness. They provided Ching-ling with the life-style of a grand lady. Her Peking residence was literally a palace, with a large number of servants. It had once been the home of the last emperor of China, who was overthrown by the 1911 revolution led by Ching-ling's husband. This mansion brought Mme Sun some criticism for enjoying luxury when many a family had only one room. But Mme Sun did not suffer a guilty conscience. She, like the other leaders of the People's Republic, never claimed to believe in egalitarianism. In old China she could have lived a hundred times more luxuriously with her family fortune or accumulated great wealth like her brothers and sisters, but she renounced all that and chose a life of austerity. She considered the wealth and extravagance of the past to be based on exploitation, which she did not consider to be the basis of her own privilege now. She enjoyed her comfort with a tranquil mind. After all, acceptable privileges in China are always associated with proper respect and status. The Communist leadership would not have been considered to have acted correctly and appropriately if it had not offered her a grand residence.

There was a definite rapport between Ching-ling and the Communist leaders. She seemed to get on well with them on a personal level. She admired Chou En-lai very much. She sometimes gave dancing parties, and would glide gracefully with him. (According to an old friend of hers: 'Mao did try. But from what I hear, wasn't very agile.')

Her relationship with Mao seemed to be rather formal. During the whole period after Liberation, she only met and talked to him privately a few times – though this was not an uncommon experience for most of the country's leaders. Mao had few personal friends. Even so, Ching-ling seems to have been relaxed with him. Mao from time to time felt great loneliness that his thought was beyond most people. Shortly before the Cultural Revolution he told the French novelist (and then Cabinet Minister) André Malraux: 'I am alone with the masses. Waiting.' He liked to quote the Chinese classics:

'If the water is too pure, no fish can survive in it.'

'If a man is too aware, no disciple can follow him.'

'The one who sings the tune of "Spring Snow" [a melody of the élite in the ancient state of Chu] is a lonely singer.'

Mao stood quite apart at the Moscow meeting in 1957; for most, his speech was both too blunt and too philosophical:

At present another situation has to be taken into account, namely, that the war maniacs may drop atomic and hydrogen bombs everywhere. They drop them and we drop them too; thus there will be chaos and lives will be lost ... How many people will die if war should break out? Out of the world's population of 2,700 million, one third – or, putting the figure a bit higher, one half – may be lost ... The other half would remain while imperialism would be razed to the ground and the whole world would become socialist. In a certain number of years, there would be 2,700 million people again and definitely more.

Virtually everybody in the hall was deeply shocked, and alarmed, by what they took to be Mao's irresponsible attitude. In his memoirs Khrushchev records that 'the audience was dead silent. No-one was prepared for such a speech.' Apparently only Ching-ling could see that Mao was talking a kind of philosophical language, in the spirit of Chinese Taoism. This philosophy places human existence in the perspective of the universe, leaving it vague whether consideration for individuals is diminished or not. Khrushchev says that Mao put the reproduction cycle rather crudely and 'allowed himself to use an indecent expression'. Ching-ling, who was sitting next to Khrushchev, 'burst out laughing at Mao's racy language. Mao laughed, too, so we all joined in with laughter.'

Ching-ling shared not only a sense of humour but also many ideals and values with her Chinese Communist colleagues. With them she shared the rocky road the People's Republic travelled, including the traumatic experience of the Cultural Revolution.

CHAPTER SEVEN

The Cultural Revolution and Last Years: 1966–81

In 1966 Ching-ling was seventy-three. In May that year Mao officially proclaimed the Cultural Revolution. In the words of the later official Party reassessment in 1981, his theory was that 'representatives of the bourgeoisie and counter-revolutionary revisionists' had taken control of the Party and the government, and the whole country had gone on to a 'capitalist road' – by which, in effect, was meant the conventional path of giving priority to economic construction. 'The cultural revolution was defined as a struggle against the revisionist line or the capitalist road.' Liu Shao-chi and Deng Xiaoping were branded heads of the 'bourgeois headquarters inside the Party' and the great majority of cadres on all levels as 'capitalist-roaders' under them.

Together with the more conventional line of the governing of the country, culture itself, Chinese and foreign, was criticized, as it was based on traditions. Mao had not forgotten his supreme dream of creating a completely new nation. Intellectuals as the epitome of culture were claimed to be the 'most stupid of all'. Everybody had to wash their brain as nobody could be free of the contamination of the old culture.

The cult of Mao was pushed to an extreme pitch. This in fact fitted in with the 2,000-year-old Chinese traditions of the absolute political and spiritual authority of the Emperor. Everybody and everything had to be scrutinized against the criteria of Mao's teachings. Unfortunately, these criteria were very vague and open to different interpretations – even though Mao himself was alive, this did not bring clarity. The whole country was plunged into chaos, with no law, no governing authority, no values and no principles. The ugly side of human beings was aroused. People kept a permanent eye on each other. They fought and killed each other in different 'Red Guard' groups, in the belief that they were making 'revolution'. Books were burnt, paintings destroyed. Long hair was 'bourgeois' and was cut on the street. So were skirts. The list of things that had to go included: flowers, pets, chess, cards, stamp-collecting, music, politeness (a professor was criticized for saying 'thank you' too often!). Everything which made life pleasant was forbidden; these things were held to stand against 'revolution' as water does against fire. What is worse was that no one knew what was permissible, or what might later be dragged up against them, or even turned against them. A composer was beaten to death for writing a song in praise of Mao – because it was similar to a traditional tune for singing to the Emperor. Constant fear of unexpected disaster was the daily companion of the Chinese population.

Ching-ling's friend, the woman writer Ting Ling, who had been kidnapped by the Kuomintang in the 1930s, was later branded as a 'Rightist' in 1957 and then spent five years in solitary confinement during the Cultural

Revolution, describes the tentacular and nerve-wracking situation:

> Under the emperors, when a man was banished, all his relatives were banished with him up to the ninth degree. We communists have done better. It's not just your relatives – even your readers are punished if your books are found in their homes. Under the emperors, repression was limited to one area. If you could flee you would be safe. Under us there is no escape. Repression covers the whole country.

In the autumn of 1966 Ching-ling was attacked by some Red Guards for being 'bourgeois': for her life-style, her love of beautiful things, her long hair and the fact that she had not joined the Communist Party. About the same time, a shrine erected to Sun Yat-sen in his native province was defaced. Sun was accused of making a 'bourgeois' revolution. Ching-ling's Shanghai house was looted. She made an allusion to the looting in 1980 when the Isaacs thanked her for giving them four wall panels as presents in the 1930s. 'It was a good thing I gave them to you! If I hadn't, they would have been destroyed!'

At the end of 1966 Ching-ling's parents' graves were desecrated. 'Were they not heads of the notorious Soong family,' said the posters beside the smashed graves, 'that had produced all these enemies of the people? Down with the Soong family!' Because of the reverence for ancestors, burial grounds were traditionally sacred to the Chinese, and destroying them was the ultimate curse on the living and the dead. This action was yet another example of the great irony of the Cultural Revolution: how the old was destroyed and replaced by the equally old.

The threat to Ching-ling was short-lived, though. The revolutionary continuity she symbolized was too important to be jeopardized. Chou En-lai, who maintained his position as premier in the Cultural Revolution largely due to his loyalty to Mao and his irreplaceable skills in managing the 'revolution'-ridden country, issued an order: 'It is absolutely forbidden to attack Comrade Soong Ching-ling.' Her parents' tombs were restored and Ching-ling was shown the photos and asked if the repairs had been done to her satisfaction. Army men were sent to guard the graveyard and her residences.

Protecting her was not an easy undertaking. Chiang Ching, who was the visible leader of the Cultural Revolution, obviously resented Mme Sun having always been the No. 1 woman leader in China – which she considered her own rightful place. In her lengthy account of women in China in her famous interviews with the American sociologist Witke, Chiang Ching never once mentioned Mme Sun's name. But for Chou's skilful handling, Chiang Ching's jealousy could have meant catastrophe – many of the vengeful woman's enemies had been persecuted and driven to suicide. Chou understood well that the only magic weapon for the protection of anyone at that time was Mao's quotations. On the hundredth anniversary of Sun Yat-sen's birth, on 12 November 1966, he quoted more than half of an entire essay by Mao on Sun written in 1956 in which Mao acknowledged Sun's historical importance. This worked.

Though she could not henceforth be harmed directly, Ching-ling was insecure and powerless. She lived in intense anxiety, hardly going out or receiving visitors, except when she was wheeled out as window-dressing at state ceremonies. Any friendship could be treated as forming an 'Anti-Party clique' and any gathering of friends could become suspect as engaging in 'counter-revolutionary activities'. Ching-ling wrote occasional notes to friends, always with the PS 'Burn this after reading.'

All her activities were either stopped or taken over. When a close colleague, the first chairman of the editorial board of *China Reconstructs*, was arrested (and subsequently driven to suicide), Ching-ling wrote later: 'I tried to reach him but failed. What was he accused of? I could get no answer.'

Isaacs wrote about the clandestine methods of communication Ching-ling used with him.

[In 1973] I sent her the Introduction to *Straw Sandals* in which I had written about her activities in the Shanghai days. After some time a note came from her, circuitously through my son . . . in Hong Kong. The note was a brief comment about *Straw Sandals*, but its real message was in its salutation, which used initials that had been part of our private code of communication during the Shanghai days. . . . Once when she had sent word that she would 'try to facilitate the visa problem,' a wire followed shortly thereafter saying 'Doctor forbids receiving friends owing influenza.' It was signed 'Suzie.' I wrote her once from India in 1975 and had no reply until one day early in 1976, a 'China Reconstructs' calendar . . . arrived in our mail at home. Clipped to one of its pages was the sliced-out piece of a letter . . . written by someone in English, that advised her sharply that I was 'a traitor' and 'never should be invited.'

Although it was extremely difficult for anyone, even her, to help other people at this time, Ching-ling did what she could for relatives, friends and colleagues. Her relatives were mainly on her mother's side. In the Cultural Revolution they belonged to the category of people 'having overseas connections', who were lumped together with other so-called 'sinister people' like landlords, rich peasants, counter-revolutionaries, Rightists, enemy agents and intellectuals. In many cases, people in this category could not even get permission to marry. Having correspondence with countries overseas was qualified as 'maintaining illicit relations with foreign enemies'. They were invariably accused of being foreign agents. Many were tortured to death. Ching-ling could not protect her relatives effectively. She could only write occasional letters and send money to tide them over difficulties.

She wrote testimonials for friends who were under suspicion. She did one for the New Zealander Rewi Alley when he was accused of being a spy – an accusation levelled against almost all foreigners in China, even those who had been 'friends of China' for many years.

Ching-ling also tried to help her Communist colleagues who were subject to the most horrifying persecutions. Liu Shao-chi was the No. 1 target of the Cultural Revolution. He was expelled from the party with the label 'a renegade, traitor and scab'. His wife was accused of being a spy for the US intelligence services. To fabricate the cases, torture was used to extract false testimony. Tens of thousands of people died under interrogation. Chiang Ching was quoted as saying: 'We must interrogate. If someone dies, let him die ... They themselves want to die. The King of Hell has invited them to drink white spirit.' Liu became seriously ill with pneumonia and diabetes. Orders were given that he be kept alive to serve as a living target for the Party's Ninth Congress, to be held in

April 1969. He died in agony shortly after the Congress was over, of medical negligence and maltreatment.

Mme Liu was thrown into prison in 1967. Ching-ling helped her children and tried to get permission for them to see their mother. She forwarded letters of entreaty from them to Mao. It was not until late 1972 that they were allowed to see their mother. In the words of the BBC correspondent Philip Short, quoting a Chinese source:

> A woman of unusual beauty, whose charm and sophistication had captivated such worldly men as President Sukarno of Indonesia, she was now 'unable to stand, her hair falling out and coughing up blood'. They broke the news to her, conveyed to them in a message from Mao a few days before, that her husband was dead.

Her children whispered in her ears the encouraging sympathy they had received, particularly from Mme Sun. Without living through those circumstances, one can hardly imagine the incredible comfort these gestures meant.

Mme Sun defended her husband more vigorously. The Cultural Revolution was a time when Mao was elevated to the place of God, and his mentors and predecessors became either defamed or non-persons. But at Sun Yat-sen's centenary meeting on 12 November 1966 Ching-ling gave a deliberately long speech – twice as long as her speech on a similar occasion ten years before. She gave a detailed account of Sun's revolutionary activities, principles and contribution. At a time when no speech was complete without shouting slogans at the end, she did not finish hers with clichés like 'Long live our great teacher, great leader, great commander and great helmsman, Chairman Mao!'

It was said that Chiang Ching tried to persuade Mme Sun to take a more active role in supporting the Cultural Revolution – but that she declined, referring to her ill-health and old age. Without doubt her personal alignments lay with the more pragmatic and moderate elements like Chou En-lai and later Deng Xiaoping.

After the fall of Mao's designated successor, Lin Piao, in the mysterious crash of a British-made Trident in Mongolia in September 1971, there was a brief period of a sort of liberalization. More moderate voices could be heard – though in a still largely oppressive atmosphere. Ching-ling came alive again. In January 1972 she published her first article for years – 'The Beginning of a New Era', on the occasion of Nixon's visit to China. She recalled Nixon's support for bombing China during the Korean War and interpreted his visit as an acknowledgement by him of defeat.

In Ching-ling's view – half wishful thinking, as with most Chinese – the ills of the Cultural Revolution seemed to have gone with Lin Piao. She started to present things in rosy colours once again.

Among the people in China there is a prevailing atmosphere and general feeling of solidarity ... Sales personnel are more attentive to their customers than ever before. Bus conductors take meticulous care of their passengers. We hear less of quarrels. Criminal cases have been reduced. Few people are sullen.

In 1973, when Chou became seriously ill with cancer, Deng was rehabilitated and by 1975 was in charge of the day-to-day work of running the country. Deng had been called 'the second biggest capitalist-roader' and had been in between house arrest and forced labour in a provincial tractor plant. His eldest son, unable to stand the daily beating-up by his fellow students at Peking University, threw himself from an upper-storey window. Nobody dared to come to his aid. He lay there for a whole day until finally being moved. But no doctors dared to treat him. He survived, but paralysed for life.

Deng was known for his pragmatism. His most famous saying was: 'It doesn't matter whether a cat is white or black. As long as it catches mice it is a good cat.' He set about trying to correct the wrongs and damage of the Cultural Revolution. Ching-ling's delight could be seen from this note she sent to a friend: 'Please accept this box of chocolate-coated cherries for you to celebrate all the victories we are having on many fronts.'

What happened then, according to the official Party re-assessment, was as follows:

Comrade Mao Zedong [Tse-tung] could not bear to accept system-atic correction of the errors of the 'Cultural Revolution' by Comrade Deng Xiaoping and triggered the movement to 'criticize Deng and counter the Right deviationist trend to reverse correct verdicts', once again plunging the nation into turmoil.

Deng was ousted again.

But by then the Chinese people were sick to the teeth with the Cultural Revolution, and had finally gathered strength to rebel. In April 1976, in the name of mourning the late premier Chou En-lai, who had died in January, there was a big spontaneous demonstration in Tien An Men square, in the heart of Peking, which was echoed all over China. These demonstrations openly signalled the people's choice for the political line of which Chou was the symbol and Deng the representative. They wanted a society free from constant crazy and repressive ideological check-ups, one which respects human dignity and gives people a decent life.

The incidents were violently suppressed. But the country continued to seethe with unrest. At the height of all this, Mao died, in September 1976. Within less than a month, Mao's wife and her group, the 'Gang of Four', were arrested without a shot being fired. The Cultural Revolution that had brought so much misery, bloodshed and death for a decade came to what seemed an incredibly easy ending, with the almost effortless disposal of a mere few.

Then came a dramatic relaxation. Almost immediately after the arrest of the Four, public demand began to call for Deng to be restored to office. 'There's no need to keep 800 million people waiting,' one wall poster complained. 'We want Deng Xiaoping to be premier right away!' 'We hope the Central Committee will make arrangements quickly, so that all hearts under heaven may be at peace,' urged another. In July 1977 Deng was officially rehabilitated again.

At first the new course was slow and tortuous. But it started to gather momentum by the end of 1978. The most dramatic thing that has happened has been the removal of fear. Chingling rejoiced at the new developments. For the occasion of 1 June, Children's Day, in 1979, she wrote a youthful article entitled 'Hello, Children!' To celebrate National Day (1 October) that year, she again wrote with exuberance 'The People's Will is Invincible':

Today, I am already over 80. But when I see that the ship of New China has been righted after being on the brink of capsizing and is now sailing magnificently forward, riding the wind and clearing the waves, no words can express my joy and happiness. Now there is hope for China.

In her last article, in February 1981, looking back on the Cultural Revolution, she urged the country 'to build socialism ... with democracy and legality, so that such abuses will never recur.'

Ching-ling was sometimes criticized for not having stood up to the horrors of the Cultural Revolution at the time. But her behaviour was consistent with her actions at the time of the Anti-Rightist Campaign in 1957, and indeed with her whole behaviour pattern in the People's Republic. Like many Communists, she was caught in her idealogical commitment. When Graham Greene visited Chungking in 1957, he commented to the mayor on the case of a famous 'counter-revolutionary', Hu Feng:

'... you will be relieved when he is at last brought to trial and you will learn whether he is guilty or innocent.'

'He must be guilty,' the Mayor replied, 'or he would never have been arrested.'

Greene and his British companions were stunned 'by the frankness of his reply'. But to the Mayor, this was the most natural thing, and it was a very widespread feeling. After the disastrous Kuomintang regime, the whole nation followed the Communists with this spontaneous single-mindedness. However, in the Cultural Revolution enthusiasm and devotion were manipulated to the extreme so that they turned into caricatures. Now the Chinese have woken up from the nightmare of the Cultural Revolution with their eyes fully opened. Many have also been hardened; they no longer have any dreams. In the turmoil of the Chinese revolution it took a strong character not to lose heart. Harold Isaacs wrote of his emotions standing in the Martyrs' Cemetery in Shanghai on his return to China in 1980:

> I stood there in the downpour, swept by a great jumble of feelings of waste and failure and anger and irony and sadness and loss coming out of the killing of the dreams of these young people and the killing of my own, mingled in half-shredded memories and the crowded overlay of nearly fifty years covering what had happened to them, and to me, in Shanghai so long ago.

When Isaacs saw Ching-ling a few months before her death, she was as committed as ever:

> ... there was to be no more time with her, I was sorry to learn, and I could only tell myself that she was fragile, unwell, and very old, and that there were still ceremonial demands that she continued to insist on meeting – the French president was coming in the next few days and she was to appear at several functions. In any case, it was clear enough that she could not or would not talk with me more about the times past, her role, her feelings about herself. A few days later ... came a note. It was written with the same bold strong strokes done with a snub-nosed pen that I first saw in the first note she ever wrote to me more than fifty years ago. 'Have been delayed with work,' it said. 'I am afraid we have to go to Outer Space for our next encounter.'

That little note summarized the predominant character of Ching-ling's long life: her bone-deep political commitment.

This was not because of a desire for power. Under the Kuomintang she could have had any post for the asking. Under the Communists she seemed to be content with her nominal position. Nor was she a seeker after fame. A few months before her death, Isaacs brought up the issue of a biography. Ching-ling 'waved the question away. No, she had never considered it, would never think of it. An American publisher had offered her half a million dollars for it, she laughed – "imagine, half a million dollars!" – but she had turned him down.' Isaacs argued. Ching-ling heard him out and 'shook her head. "No," she said again, and very plainly closed the subject.'

She even subordinated Sun Yat-sen's name to her general course. Even though the Communists, unlike the Kuomintang, largely ignored Sun, she still chose the former group. She kept her feelings to herself until almost her last days, when she said to Isaacs: 'After all, to bring down an empire was no small thing.'

Had she been less dedicated, she could have led a comfortable exile's life. Instead, she was always struggling in the depth of whirlpools out of her own choice. Ching-ling sacrificed a great deal for her political commitment, not least her relationship with her family. She was a very family-conscious woman. The place of honour on the wall of the dining-room in her Shanghai residence was given to an oil portrait of her mother (in China the placing of portraits is of great significance). In a five-page letter to a friend about Edgar Snow's account of her life in *Journey to the Beginning*, one thing she was very upset about was Snow's claim that her parents had disowned her after her marriage.

It must have been extremely hard for her to be in constant bitter battles with her family, although she never gave even a hint that this was so. Whatever their political differences, it must have been painful to see her sister Mei-ling's name put up by the Communists next to Chiang Kai-shek's as the 'No. 1 wanted war criminal', and to see the Soong family designated as one of the 'four big notorious families'. No less painful must have been the bitter blows dealt to her and her friends by her own family, and especially her brother-in-law, Chiang. All this meant that her life must at times have been lonely – and this was not eased by the fact that as the 'Mother of China', in a very status-conscious society, she was on a pedestal.

Perhaps this is why she formed close friendships with a number of foreigners. They treated her more like an equal than most Chinese did. Commenting on her paintings, which were made into hangings and souvenirs, one of her foreign friends said with a smile – in a way few Chinese would: 'I know she played around with brushes, but I don't know what her "paintings" were like.'

She was apparently also fond of a couple of young people who did not behave in her presence with conventional reverence and awe. It must have been a relief for her to be able to relax and it was not easy to find people with whom she could do so.

Quite late in life she adopted two very young girls. As Isaacs observed in 1980: 'now old enough to be a great grandmother, [she] had clearly snatched from her circumstances some of what it was like to be a mother.' Apparently the two girls were very close to her heart and she had the reputation of spoiling them. In spite of the affection she lavished on them, they do not seem to have taken after her. An American journalist, Fox Butterfield, recalled seeing the elder daughter in the Peking Hotel:

She was dressed in a short, hip-hugging wool skirt, high brown-leather boots, and a bright-orange blouse ... She had on heavy eye shadow and lipstick: not pretty, but haughty, striking, and sexy. She looked like a movie star from Taiwan or Hong Kong. I noticed her often after that, on her way to the beauty parlor in the hotel or driving in her Red Flag to the evening movies at the International Club, reserved for foreigners.

A middle-aged Chinese woman who worked in the movie industry commented to Butterfield: 'She will be a movie star until Madame Sun dies. Then it's all over.'

Ching-ling endured a 56-year-long widowhood. When Sun Yat-sen died in 1925, she was thirty-two – in the prime of her beauty and with what Helen Snow noticed was a 'saucy' side to her and

by nature super-feminine with all that term implies ... she was by nature a woman who was not qualified to stand alone in an ugly and hostile world. Nature intended that she should be loved and protected by a Sun Yat-sen instead of being left to fight his battle for him. She was intended by nature to be a wife, not a Joan of Arc – and she knew it.

She had a great number of admirers, both Chinese and foreign. Nehru was fascinated with her after he first met her in Moscow in 1927, as he wrote to his sister. Western journalists went away infatuated. Isaacs was one of them. A passage by him fifty years later is poignant:

If this sketch suggests that I was smitten, it is because I was. I was smitten hard by this beautiful great lady, as who could not have been, it seemed to me then, and seems so to me now. If there are no warts on this miniature portrait, it is because I never saw any, and if there were any I was not seeing, I am just as glad. I was twenty-one and, as I have amply indicated, enormously impressionable; she was about forty and enormously impressive as a woman and as a person. For her beauty, her courage, her queenly espousal of just causes, I came to love her like a young knight pure in heart. In return she bestowed on me an ever correct yet warmly personal affection. Make what one might of that now, that is how it was.

On the matter of love, they never exchanged a single word, except fifty years later, at their re-encounter in 1980:

'But I want to tell you, Suzie,' I plunged on, 'the one thing I do carry with me as precious from that time in Shanghai was the love I had for you.' Soong Ching-ling looked at me with a face I could not read. She half-closed her eyes and in her soft hoarse voice said, 'I am honored.'

Not least because of her outstanding beauty and pronounced femininity, Ching-ling was followed all her days by stories about her private life. Under the Kuomintang, according to Isaacs:

she became the target of scurrilous gossip used as a deliberate weapon against her and many friends with whom she became identified in politics during those turbulent years. I remember once, when the latest such bit appeared in what was called the 'mosquito press' in Shanghai in the Kuomintang days ... she said to me in a rueful half-jest: 'They've had me in affairs with all these men and I've never had a single moment's pleasure out of any of it!'

In her later years there was speculation that she had a lover – some say her secretary – and what was more, that the affair was sanctioned by the Communist leadership. The story was vigorously brushed aside by some of Ching-ling's friends in China as 'slander from the Gang of Four'. But ordinary Chinese folk did not see the suggestion as defaming her image. The legend was more a typical Chinese device: it designed a solution for the blemish in something that was otherwise perfect. They regarded it as a pity for Mme Sun to endure a life of half a century of widowhood; but they did not want her to marry somebody else. By tradition the Chinese favour the satisfaction of human senses and feelings. They also value proper performance of duty. In addition, they prefer a happy ending to be brought about by a human hand from above – in this case the Communist leadership.

But all this remains speculation. It is actually more likely that Mme Sun guarded herself with painstaking prudence against any possible scandal. She was not a heart-broken wife devoted to her deceased husband, nor a virtuous widow protecting her impeccable reputation. She was married to her ideals and did not want to risk endangering them by giving her enemies any chance to blacken her name, however unjustifiably.

Ching-ling made her last public appearance on 8 May 1981, to receive an Honorary Doctorate of Law from Victoria University, Canada. Four days later she wrote her last words – an inscription for a book of manuscripts of Chou Tao-jen, one of the 'Seven Gentlemen'. The next day, the illness which she had suffered from for two decades, chronic lymphocytic leukaemia, worsened. Her condition deteriorated rapidly. On the 15th Mme Chou En-lai visited her and delivered the news that she had been inducted into the Communist Party. On the 16th she was named Honorary President of the People's Republic.

It is hard to say whether she was fully aware of these 'last rites'. But she probably would have consented if she were, as her whole life had shown a total commitment to co-operating with the Communist Party.

On 29 May 1981 she succumbed to leukaemia in Peking at the age of eighty-eight. She had given instructions early that year to be interred in the family burial ground in Shanghai, next to her parents and her life-long servant. She did not want to be in the Sun Yat-sen Mausoleum. Her close colleagues say that this was because she did not want a fuss made over her death. Some also recall her intense dislike of the Mausoleum which she saw as Chiang Kai-shek's work. Whatever the reason, with this decision Ching-ling told the world that she was not Caesar's widow, but an independent fighter. Though the ideals for which she fought so hard and so long were often couched in the name of Dr Sun Yat-sen, they were very much her own.

Her legacy is a resolute devotion to her principles – not a devotion which was shut in on itself but one that spread warmth and hope.

SELECT BIBLIOGRAPHY

The main source on Ching-ling's life up to 1940 is Emily Hahn's *The Soong Sisters* (New York, Doubleday, 1941; London, Robert Hale, 1942), though this concentrates more on Mei-ling and Ai-ling than on Ching-ling. Roby Eunson, *The Soong Sisters* (New York, Franklin Watts, 1975), is a brief work which adds little to what is in Hahn. The only person to whom Ching-ling gave an interview was Edgar Snow, in the early 1930s: he records it in *Journey to the Beginning* (London, Gollancz, 1960; New York, Random House, 1972). There is an unforgettable portrayal of Ching-ling in Wuhan and Moscow in 1927 in Vincent Sheean's *Personal History* (New York, Garden City Publishing Co. Inc., 1937). Harold Isaacs, an old friend and colleague from the early 1930s in Shanghai, provides a fascinating and unique account of meeting Ching-ling again in 1980, with flashbacks to earlier periods, in his *Re-Encounters in China: Notes of a Journey in a Time Capsule* (Armonk, NY, and London, M. E. Sharpe, 1985). Helen Foster Snow (Nym Wales), *Women in Modern China* (The Hague, Mouton, and New York, Humanities Press, 1967), has a long section on Ching-ling, based on close acquaintance with her in the 1930s and on unpublished materials of Edgar Snow. Sterling Seagrave, *The Soong Dynasty* (New York, Harper & Row; London, Sidgwick & Jackson, 1985), is racy and informative; though basically sympathetic to Ching-ling, it does not focus on her and says very little about her. The special supplement on Ching-ling in the September 1981 issue of *China Reconstructs*, the magazine she founded, contains many details and useful reminiscences from her closest colleagues and friends.

Many of Ching-ling's key essays and pronouncements are collected together in the volume Soong Ching-ling, *The Struggle for New China* (Peking, Foreign Languages Press, 1952); however, this is a selection and only covers the years 1927–52; her later texts were mainly published in *China Reconstructs*. Other important texts are available in a Chinese collection, *Soong Ching-ling Xuan Ji* (*Selected Works of Soong Ching-ling*) (Peking, People's Publishing House, 1966). There is a rich photographic album, with a detailed chronology and useful information in the captions: *Ji-nian Soong Ching-ling Tong-zhi* (*In Memory of Comrade Soong Ching-ling*) (Peking, Wen-wu Publishing Co., 1982). Also in Chinese, there is a short biography, *Soong Ching-ling* (Hong Kong, Wide Angle Publishing House, 1981).

Many people who met Ching-ling left descriptions of her, often very touching ones. Among the most illuminating for the earlier years are those of Sun Yat-sen's bodyguard in Charles Drage, *The Life and Times of General Two-Gun Cohen* (New York, Funk & Wagnalls, and London, Jonathan Cape, 1954); Vera Vladimirovna Vishnyakova-Akimova, *Two Years in Revolutionary China 1925-1927* (Cambridge, Mass., Harvard University East Asia Research Center, 1971); Percy Chen (son of Foreign Minister Eugene Chen), *China Called Me: My Life Inside the Chinese Revolution* (Boston, Little Brown, 1979); and Anna Louise Strong, *China's Millions: The Revolutionary Struggles from 1927 to 1935* (London, Gollancz, 1936). Harrison Salisbury, *To Peking – and Beyond: A Report on the New Asia* (New York, Quadrangle/New York Times, 1973) contains a rare description of Ching-ling in 1972.